A New

MW00612348

Dick B.'s Reference Titles on Alcoholics Anonymous History
Paradise Research Publications, Inc., Publisher;
Good Book Publishing Company, Distributor P.O. Box 837, Kihei, HI 96753-0837
Phone/Fax: (808) 874 4876; Email: dickb@dickb.com; URL: http://www.dickb.com/index.shtml

Publisher's June 1, 2006 List of Titles by Author Dick B.

Anne Smith's Journal, 1933-1939.

By the Power of God: A Guide to Early A.A. Groups & Forming Similar Groups Today.

Cured!: Proven Help for Alcoholics and Addicts.

Dr. Bob and His Library.

God and Alcoholism: Our Growing Opportunity in the 21st Century.

Good Morning!: Quiet Time, Morning Watch, Meditation, and Early A.A

Henrietta B. Seiberling: Ohio's Lady with a Cause.

Making Known The Biblical History and Roots of Alcoholics Anonymous: An Fifteen-Year Research, Writing, Publishing and Fact Dissemination Project.

New Light on Alcoholism: God, Sam Shoemaker, and A.A

The Akron Genesis of Alcoholics Anonymous.

The Books Early AAs Read for Spiritual Growth

The Conversion of Bill W.

The First Nationwide A.A. History Conference - Comments of Dick B.

The Golden Text of A.A.: God, the Pioneers, and Real Spirituality.

The Good Book and The Big Book: A.A.'s Roots in the Bible.

The Good Book-Big Book Guidebook.

The James Club: The Original A.A. Program's Absolute Essentials.

The Oxford Group & Alcoholics Anonymous.

That Amazing Grace (Clarence & Grace S.).

Turning Point: A History of Early A.A.'s Spiritual Roots and Successes.

Twelve Steps for You: Let Our Creator, A.A. History, and the Big Book Be Your Guide.

Utilizing Early A.A.'s Spiritual Roots for Recovery Today.

When Early AA s Were Cured and Why.

Why Early A.A. Succeeded: The Good Book in Alcoholics Anonymous Yesterday and Today (a Bible Study Primer)

Available through other distributors

Hope: The Story of Geraldine O. Delaney, 2d ed. (Alina Lodge)
Our Faith Community A.A. Legacy (Dick B., ed and compiler).
　(Came to Believe Publications)
Courage to Change (with Bill Pittman). (Hazelden)
Women Pioneers of AA (Dick B., contributor). (Hazelden)

A New Way Out

New Path - Familiar Road Signs - Our Creator's Guidance

Dick B.

Paradise Research Publications, Inc.
Kihei, Maui, Hawaii

Paradise Research Publications, Inc.
PO Box 837
Kihei, HI 96753-0837
(808 874 4876)
Email: dickb@dickb.com
URL: http://www.dickb.com/index.shtml

© 2006 by Anonymous
All rights reserved. Published 2006.
Printed in the United States of America

Cover Design: Terry Dunford (American Creations of Maui)

This Paradise Research Publications Edition is published by arrangement with Good Book Publishing Company, PO Box 837, Kihei, HI: 96753-0837

The publication of this volume does not imply affiliation with, nor approval or endorsement from Alcoholics Anonymous World Services, Inc. The views expressed herein are solely those of the author. A.A. is a program of recovery from alcoholism–use of the Twelve Steps in connection with programs and activities which are patterned after A.A. but which address other problems, does not imply otherwise.

Note: All Bible verses quoted in this book, unless otherwise noted, are from the Authorized (or "King James") Version. The letters "KJV" are used when necessary to distinguish it from other versions.

ISBN 1-885803-89-3

Contents

A New Way Out

New Path - Familiar Road Signs - Our Creator's Guidance

Dick B.

An introductory chapter for all those dedicated servants, organizations, professionals, and still-suffering individuals who want to know how our Creator reached into one of the great social movements of our age, touched the lives of its founders and members, and enabled them to ask His guidance along a path—a way out—that would deliver those who wanted to become His children, to seek His power and strength, to obey His rules, and to prove Him with their healed minds and bodies and glorify Him with their love and service to Him and bring others into His family with faith, hope, and love.

Simple Instructions

Ask our Heavenly Father the Way
Become one of His children
Tell others what He has done for you and will do for others in trouble
Pray to Him and for them and show them how to pray
Study His Word as a lamp for your feet
Claim the love, power, strength, and deliverance He offers
Program your life to glorify Him - with love for Him and others
Carve out time for personal work with newcomers

Historical documentation of victories available to young people who want to pray; to organizations that want to use their evangelistic efforts anew; to movements seeking effective help for alcoholics, addicts, and others with life-controlling problems; and to all who want to establish a relationship with the Creator, learn from the Bible, talk to and hear from Him, and walk in fellowship with Him, His Son, and like-minded believers and let Him make them free.

Playing God's Game of the Royal Way

[Brother Andrew was called "God's Smuggler" because of his courageous delivery of Bibles to the persecuted in countries where such activity meant death and imprisonment. As a missionary student, he had been told: "The real purpose of this training is to teach our students that they can trust God to do what He h has said He would do." Time and time again, in spite of obstacles and reversals, God miraculously met the needs of His servant, whose stories of brothers and sisters in the body of Christ ask: "How big is your Kingdom? How big is your God?" (Brother Andrew. *The Narrow Road: Stories of Thos Who Walk This Road Together*. MI: Fleming H. Revell, 2002)

What God has told us He would do

In God I have put my trust: I will not be afraid what man can do unto me
Psalm 55:11

Hear my prayer, O God: give ear to the words of my mouth
Psalm 54:2

Teach me thy way, O LORD. I will walk in thy truth: unite my heart to fear thy name
Psalm 86:11

Commit thy way unto the LORD; trust also in him; and he shall bring it to pass
Psalm37:5

Trust in the LORD with all thine heart; and lean not unto thine own understanding. In all thy ways acknowledge him, and he shall direct thy paths
Proverbs 3:5-6

x

This poor man cried, and the LORD heard him, and saved him out of
all his troubles
Psalm 34:6

Now Samuel did not yet know the LORD, neither was the word of the
LORD yet revealed unto Him. And the LORD called Samuel again the
third time. And he arose and went to Eli, and said, Here am I; for thou
didst call me. And Eli perceived that the LORD had called the child.
Therefore Eli said unto Samuel, Go, lie down: and it shall be, if he call
thee, thou shalt say, Speak, LORD for thy servant heareth
1 Samuel 3:7-9

There was a man of the Pharisees, named Nicodemus, a ruler of the
Jews: The same came to Jesus by night, and said unto him, Rabbi, we
know that thou art a teacher come from God: for no man can do these
miracles that thou doest, except God be with him. Jesus answered and
said unto him, Verily, verily I say unto thee, Except a man be born
again, he cannot see the kingdom of God
John 3:1-3

For God so loved the world, that he gave his only begotten Son, that
whosoever believeth in him should not perish, but have everlasting life
John 3:16

Thomas saith unto him, Lord, we know not whither thou goest; and
how can we know the way? Jesus saith unto him, I am the way, the
truth, and the life: no man cometh unto the Father but by me.
John 14:5-6

And he [Saul] trembling and astonished said, Lord, what wilt thou
have me to do? And the Lord said unto him, Arise, and go into the
city, and it shall be told thee what thou must do.
Acts 9:6

Moreover, brethren, I declare unto you the gospel which I preached
unto you, which also ye have received, and wherein ye stand. By
which also ye are saved, if ye keep in memory what I preached unto
you, unless ye have believed in vain. For I delivered unto you first of

all that which I received, how that Christ died for our sins according to the scriptures; And that he was buried, and that he rose again the third day according to the scriptures; And that he was seen of Cephas, then of the twelve.
1 Corinthians 15:1-5

Then Peter said unto them, Repent, and be baptized every one of you in the name of Jesus Christ for the remission of sins, and ye shall receive the gift of the Holy Ghost
Acts 2:38

God's Will

Let us hear the conclusion of the whole matter: Fear God, and keep his commandments: for this is the whole duty of man. Ecclesiastes 12:13

For this is good and acceptable in the sight of God our Saviour; Who will have all men to be saved, and to come unto the knowledge of the truth. 1 Timothy 2:3-4

A New Way Out

New Path - Familiar Road Signs - Our Creator's Guidance

A New Way To Travel A Well-Lighted Path to Recovery, Healing, and Wholeness While Effectively Reckoning with Prejudices against Religious Means on the One Hand, and Prejudices Against 12-Step Programs on the Other

A New Way Out of Jails and Correctional Facilities, Alcoholism, Addiction, Life-Controlling Problems, Homelessness, Abandonment, Abuse, Dependency, Fear, Self-condemnation, Hopelessness, and Despair

When this title speaks of "A New Way Out," it speaks of a way out of correctional facilities and prisons, a way out of alcoholism and addictions, a way out of life-controlling problems, and a way out of the prisons of the mind that bind people to fear, self-condemnation, and despair. We speak to "God's way out." We take our cue from the Bible. But we urge the reader to heed 1 Thessalonians 5:21: "Prove all things; hold fast that which is good." (*King James Version*)

The Bible on "A Way Out"

". . . . No temptation has seized you except what is common to man. And God is faithful; he will not let you be tempted beyond what you can bear, he also will provide *a way out* so that you can stand up under it." (1 Corinthians 10:11, *Comparative Study Bible*, Rev ed. New International Version. MI: Zondervan, 1999, p. 2929, italics added)

"Trust in the LORD with all thine heart; and lean not unto thine own understanding. In all thy ways acknowledge him, and he shall direct thy paths. Proverbs 3:5-6

Alcoholics Anonymous Language

"According to a letter dated July 18, 1939. . . Bill, at that time, was using 'Alcoholics Anonymous' both as a working title of the book [A.A.'s basic text] and as a name of the fellowship. Among other titles suggested were. . . 'The Way Out' . . . The choices quickly boiled down to 'The Way Out,' favored by a majority in Akron, and 'Alcoholics Anonymous,' preferred by most in New York. When a vote was taken in the two groups, 'The Way Out' prevailed by a bare majority. . . . The Library of Congress had 25 books entitled 'The Way Out,' 12 entitled, 'The Way,' and none called 'Alcoholics Anonymous.' That settled the matter; nobody wanted to struggle with the burden of being simply another 'way out'." (*Pass In On*. NY: Alcoholics Anonymous World Services, Inc., 1984, pp. 202-203)

1.

Directions for The New Way Out

History is our product. It's what we are marketing. It's what we offer to you and urge you to include in your own way out of suffering. Suffering from abandonment, addictions, alcoholism, dependency, despair, fear, homelessness, hopelessness, jail, imprisonment, and the prisons of your mind.

Where do we start? With what's gone wrong? With past mistakes? With what's not working? With competing ideas and programs? With the magnitude of the problem? Or with the solution? A solution that puts before you, and which you should put before others, that provides you with an accurate, comprehensive, complete account of exactly what has worked, where it came from, what ideas it incorporated, and what principles and practices it used.

Go To the Father First

You seldom look at a book or article, listen to a scholarly lecture, or watch a TV or talk show without hearing of some new wonder-program, some new drug, some new scientific discovery, or some new professional's viewpoint that tells you how to solve your problem. But is it from God? Did the writer or speaker talk to God first? Does it fit within the practices, principles, and promises in God's Word? Does it tell you what God wants, or what the speaker or writer wants, or what you want? The point here is that, if you want to play the Royal Way Game, and if you want to receive the benefits of traveling the narrow road, you need to take it up with the Creator first.

Look At The Early A.A. Christian Fellowship For Clues

I've just completed twenty-nine historical books on every conceivable aspect of early A.A. history and successes. Early A.A.'s solution to

1

life's problems was reliance on the Creator. It produced a 75% success rate in Akron, and a 93% success rate in Cleveland among the medically incurable alcoholics who really tried. And that's a model worth learning. It was simple. It was effective. And it attracted adherents and promoted growth because it worked.

We will have much more to say about the early program and how to use it today. But first, let's get it before us. It happens that John D. Rockefeller, Jr. also had the same objective. Bill Wilson had come to him looking for money. Bill described the results Dr. Bob and his helpers were achieving in Akron. And Rockefeller decided to see for himself. So he sent his agent Frank Amos over to Akron, and Amos reported back in two different papers exactly what he had found. He had spent about a week in Akron, interviewed Dr. Bob and members of his fellowship, interviewed their wives, interviewed judges, attorneys, medical colleagues, and others. And the following is the essence of the program Amos said was working so well:

- An alcoholic must realize that he is an alcoholic, incurable from a medical viewpoint, and that he must never drink anything with alcohol in it.
- He must surrender himself absolutely to God, realizing that in himself there is no hope.
- Not only must he want to stop drinking permanently, he must remove from his life other sins such as hatred, adultery, and others which frequently accompany alcoholism. Unless he will do this absolutely, Smith and his associates refuse to work with him.
- He must have devotions every morning–a "quiet time" of prayer and some reading from the Bible and other religious literature. Unless this is faithfully followed, there is grave danger of backsliding.
- He must be willing to help other alcoholics get straightened out. This throws up a protective barrier and strengthens his own willpower and convictions.
- It is important, but not vital, that he meet frequently with other reformed alcoholics and form both a social and a religious comradeship.
- Important, but not vital, that he attend some religious service at least once weekly.

Of those seven points, the last two—religious comradeship and church attendance—were simply recommended, but not required. The program had no steps—twelve, six, or otherwise. It had no basic text but the Bible. For reading matter, it made a great many Christian books and articles available on circulation.

Completeness dictates that we describe the Akron Christian Fellowship and its work a little more fully because it involved some additional matters Amos didn't cover. Here, therefore, is the original program as reconstructed from all our historical resources.

An Overview of What They Did in Akron

Hospitalization for about seven days: Hospitalization and/or medical help for a brief period was virtually a "must" for most early A.A. members. During that period, only a Bible was allowed in the hospital room; medications were administered; there were daily visits and lengthy talks by Dr. Bob with the patients; there were visits by the recovered pioneers who told of their victories; there was an acknowledgement of belief in the Creator, a "surrender" to Christ, a prayer; and then release.

Recovery in the homes: Recovery work in Akron did not take place in groups or meetings or treatment centers; nor in rehabs or therapy or confinement. It took place primarily in homes, and that in itself constituted a very different situation than the one found in the Oxford Group as such. In the homes, there were: (1) Daily get-togethers. (2) Bible studies and reading. (3) Individual quiet times. (4) Quiet time meetings in the Smith home in the morning with Dr. Bob's wife Anne. (5) Discussions with Dr. Bob, Henrietta Seiberling, and Anne Smith. (6) A regular Wednesday meeting with "Real" surrenders upstairs after the manner of James 5:15-16 with "elders" and prayer, acceptance of Jesus Christ, asking God to take alcohol out of their lives, and asking Him to help them live by the Four Absolutes. (7) Utilization of some Oxford Group life-changing practices such as Inventory, Confession, Conviction, and Restitution. (8) Arranging visits to newcomers at the hospital. (9) Recommended church attendance by most. (10) Social, religious, and family fellowship.

The Regular Wednesday Meeting: There were no significant Oxford Group testimonials or alcoholic drunkalogs. There was a set-up meeting on Mondays where leaders sought God's guidance as to topics and leaders for the Wednesday meeting. The regular meeting involved an opening prayer; reading of Scripture; group prayer and seeking of guidance; discussion led by someone such as Dr. Bob, Henrietta Seiberling, or T. Henry Williams; "real" surrenders upstairs for the newcomers; arranging visits to the hospital; closing with the Lord's Prayer; socializing; and the exchange of Christian literature. No drunkalogs. No Steps. No Big Book. No texts at all. Just the Bible and devotionals like *The Upper Room.*

Quiet Times: (held by individuals, by the group, and by the early birds in the morning with Anne Smith). The first condition of receiving revelation is *not* "listening" to God. It is becoming a child of God by accepting Jesus Christ as Lord and Saviour. Hence, this was a vital part of the Akron program–evidenced by the "surrender" at the hospital and often the "real surrender" in the homes. Then, for born-again believers, Quiet Time consisted of reading the Bible, prayer to and seeking guidance from God, use of devotionals like *The Upper Room,* utilizing Anne Smith's Journal for teaching and instruction, and reading Christian literature such as Henry Drummond's *The Greatest Thing in the World* and Nora Smith Holm's *The Runner's Bible..*

The Emphasis of Bob and Bill together: I have several times quoted or summarized the statements of Bob and Bill together on the platform of the Shrine Auditorium in Los Angeles in 1943. The remarks were reported in the March, 1943 issue of *The Tidings.* About 4500 AAs and their families were present. Bill spoke about the importance of Divine Aid, the religious element in A.A., and prayer. Dr. Bob spoke about the importance of cultivating the habit of prayer and reading the Bible. Both men were warmly received–a testimony to their harmonious accord, consistency, and simplicity of presentation when appearing together.

Looking at Prior, Long-standing, Transforming Programs For
The Homeless, Despondent, At-risk, Criminal, Alcoholic, and Addicted

- **The Salvation Army (Founded in the 1870's):** Whose founder General Booth said "the first vital step in saving outcasts consists in making them feel that some decent human being cares enough for them to take an interest in the question whether they are to rise or to sink." Advocating: (1) Abstinence. (2) Salvation and Reliance on God. (3) Fellowship among those who understand. (4) The opportunity to work with those suffering the same difficulty. (5) Faith in the ability of the individual and the power of God to accomplish the desired ends. The importance of the Salvation Army to A.A. was underlined by a plan of Bill Wilson's to donate all royalty money from the Big Book over expenses to institutions like the Salvation Army "that would help alcoholics indirectly" (letter Henrietta Seiberling to John Seiberling Jr., dated October 23, 1945).

- **Christian Endeavor International (Founded in 1881 by Rev. Francis E. Clark, in Williston, Vermont)**: Bringing the youth back to supporting their local church through love and service, and pledging. (1) Confession of Christ. (2) Prayer. (3) Bible study, (4) Conversion meetings. (5) Quiet Hour and, (6) Christian and social fellowship with believers—its top membership: 3,500,000, with worldwide impact.

- **The Gospel and Rescue Missions (First founded in August, 1872, at Jerry McAuley's Water Street Mission, in New York):** Offering shelter, food, clothing, opportunity for de-lousing, and a warm place to sleep. Promising release from addictions through rehabilitation, as well as their versions of spiritual healing and salvation. Grounded on Salvation: (1) There was the Gospel Meeting with hymns; singing; reading from the Bible; testimony of the leader as to how he was saved from gambling, alcohol, and sin; testimony from converts and the audience; (2) Then followed the altar call inviting, with appropriate song, those "almost persuaded" to go forward, accompanied by a worker who tells the newcomer how Christ saved and cleansed him; and helps the penitent to say a prayer, however short or faltering; (3) The penitent's experience of a powerful emotional experience of forgiveness, release, and exaltation; (4) Providing—for those who attend—food and shelter, and, for those staying longer because of possibility of permanent recovery, efforts to locate employment, reconcile with families, and receive personal counseling; (5) Expecting the convert to do small jobs, attend regular Bible study, prayer, and gospel meetings, and later on to testify. Serving the homeless, mentally ill wandering the streets, and chemically dependent—chronically unemployed and unemployable, sporadic workers, and those "on the bum." In a little noticed remark about the writing of the Big Book, Bill pointed out that A.A.'s southern friend, Fitz M., "wanted a fairly religious book infused with some of the dogma we had picked up from the churches and missions which had tried to help us." (Bill W., "Where did the 12 Steps come from?" July 1953 *A.A. Grapevine*).

- **Young Men's Christian Association (Founded in London, 1844 by George Williams and a group of Evangelical Christians as a substitute for Bible study and prayer on the streets)**. YMCA is the largest not-for-profit community organization in the U.S. with 2594 Y's and 20.1 million members. Originally for helping young men build a healthy spirit, mind, and body in Christian discipleship through a program of religious, educational, social, and physical activities. Emphasizing: (1) Education. (2) Physical fitness. (3) Parent/child activities; (4) Spiritual growth, particularly stressing Bible study.

- **The Oxford Group (Organized about 1919 as "A First Century Christian Fellowship" by Rev. Frank N. D. Buchman, a Lutheran Minister and his friends):** Utilizing "God's art" of changing lives through a specific program employing 1) Belief in, and obedience to God. (2) Surrender to God; (3) Eliminating sin by Inventory, Confession, Conviction, Conversion, and Continuance; (4) Making Restitution; (5) Quiet Time with Bible study, prayer, seeking God's guidance, using devotionals; (6) Fellowship; (7) Witness; and (8) Resultant Spiritual Experience. Their slogan: Sin, the Problem; Christ the cure; Miracle, the result.

- **Early A.A.'s Pioneer Akron Christian Fellowship (Founded on June 10, 1935 by Bill W. and Dr. Bob in Akron, Ohio):** Their spiritual recovery program required (1) Abstinence; (2) Hospitalization; (3) Accepting Christ; (4) Resisting Temptation; (5) Relying on and Obeying the Creator; (6)

6

Eliminating Sin; (7) Growing in Fellowship through Bible study, prayer, Quiet Time, and Christian literature; (8) Passing on to others the simple message that they too must help others in order to stay well. (9) Living in the homes of other alcoholics while getting well and on their feet.

History Shows Some Major, Common Elements of Success in Akron's Fellowship and in Those Great Movements That Went Before

The following appear to be the common elements:

- Individual participants who had suffered and overcome the same difficulties as the new person and gave evidence of caring about the deliverance of the latter, usually without any personal gain whatsoever.

- New entrants willing to go to any lengths to achieve victory and really try to follow directions.

- Commitment to permanent abstinence—whatever the nature of the sin or excess.

- Reliance on the Creator for guidance, strength, and help; and coming to Him through acceptance of His son Jesus Christ.

- Obedience to the Creator's will; avoidance of temptation; elimination of sinful conduct associated with old behavior—whether alcohol, drugs, crime, etc.

- Growth in fellowship with the Creator, His son, and other believers through Bible study, prayer, seeking guidance in Quiet Times, and studying helpful devotionals and literature.

- Sharing bed, board, shelter, religious, and social activities with other believers, frequently living in, or frequenting the homes of recovered individuals in better straits.

- Receiving mature counseling from successful individuals on proper behavior, nutrition, employment, education, and good health needed for successful re-entry.

- Devotion to loving and serving—usually without charge--those still afflicted, and by apprising them in personal stories of what God had done for the veterans that they could not do for themselves.

Talking With the Creator About Amplifying Your Program By Including This History

["**For my thoughts are not your thoughts, neither are your ways my ways, saith the LORD. For as the heavens are higher than the earth, so are my ways higher than your ways, and my thoughts than your thoughts" Isaiah 55:8-9"**]

Have You Talked With The Creator?

I have firmly concluded—from my own 20 years of experience as an active member of Alcoholics Anonymous, my own sponsorship of more than 100 men in recovery, and my own 17 years of research into the history of A.A.— that the greatest difficulties today in all recovery programs arise from a lack of information about A.A. roots, a lack historical knowledge about those prior, successful recovery programs which placed their works in God's hands, an unwillingness to consider the successes of early movements and of early A.A., a conviction that man's ways can do the job, and an utter failure to ask the questions so often asked in early A.A.: What does it say in the Good Book? What does the Creator want me to do? What would the Master say? Why are our own plans and efforts bearing so little fruit?

Have You Asked Him How To Proceed?

There are pertinent questions: Have you asked our Heavenly Father for help? Have you talked to Him about your problems? Have you asked the Creator what He wishes to have you do?

Let's look at some recovery history. Let's see if any person or group has actually placed a proposed program of Divine Aid before the Divine Creator and followed His suggestions.

2.

Additional History on Programs That Have Gone Before

Bill Wilson's 12 Step Spiritual Kindergarten

Alcoholics Anonymous was founded on June 10, 1935. And that event ushered in a whole era of dynamic programs and a long-overdue renewed focus on spiritual means of recovery from alcoholism, addiction, and other life-controlling problems.

A.A.'s spiritual solution expanded from Alcoholics Anonymous to an estimated 200 other "anonymous" recovery groups. Also to other "Twelve Step" groups. Then to other not-so-anonymous recovery groups and meetings in churches, non-profit agencies, and government facilities. Then to addiction prevention and treatment programs in rehabs, hospitals, in-patient and outpatient treatment facilities; then to self-help groups, mutual support groups, and therapy. Then to widespread publishing of "official" texts, guidebooks, recovery books, treatises, research papers, and scientific investigations. And inevitably to research and history societies, grants and funding, and alternative therapies. And then even into so-called Recovery Bibles which published Bibles that included Twelve Step phrases and language, meditation ideas, and psychological materials.

The variety of ever-proliferating spiritual and other recovery programs patterned on, or derived from, Alcoholics Anonymous and its Twelve Steps, can today be found in such organizations as the Salvation Army, Rescue Missions, the Veterans Administration, Branches of the U.S. Military, church and youth organizations, Teen Challenge, Overcomers Outreach, Inc, Celebrate Recovery, Alcoholics for Christ, and Alcoholics Victorious. Most have used, modified, or dramatically changed the Twelve Step recovery ideas—and certainly the early A.A.

11

Christian Fellowship program in Akron that preceded the whole shebang.

Yet, as A.A. co-founder Bill Wilson claimed so often, nobody "invented" A.A., and it was, as Bill characterized it, just a "spiritual kindergarten" Bill claimed its ideas came from religion, medicine, and the experience of alcoholics themselves. Co-founder Dr. Bob declared that the basic ideas came from study and effort in the Bible— particularly the Book of James, the Sermon on the Mount, and 1 Corinthians 13. Both Bill Wilson and Dr. Bob acknowledged a debt to the Oxford Group (later called Moral Re-Armament and also called "A First Century Christian Fellowship") for the "terse and tangible" program of action embodied in A.A.'s Big Book and Twelve Steps. Both said Jesus' Sermon on the Mount contained A.A.'s underlying philosophy.

The Many, Varied, Diverse Sources of Bill's Twelve Step Program

Historical research since 1990 has unearthed, defined, and articulated a large number of ideas that reached A.A. from the King James Version of the Bible, United Christian Endeavor Society, Young Men's Christian Association; The Salvation Army; rescue missions; Dr. Frank Buchman's Oxford Group; The Rev. Sam Shoemaker's role and teachings from the Bible and the Oxford Group; a core idea from Dr. Carl Gustav Jung; some core ideas and language from Professor William James of Harvard; the extensive work with alcoholics by Dr. William Duncan Silkworth—primarily at Towns Hospital; the literature and practices with Christian Quiet Time and meditation books and devotionals popular in the 1930's; the specific teachings of Anne Ripley Smith (wife of Dr. Bob)—found initially in the spiritual journal she kept and shared in the 1930's; several psychological ideas from lay therapist Richard Peabody; a number of words and ideas from "New Thought" proponents such as Ralph Waldo Trine, Emmet Fox, Christian Science, and Unity; and a large body of literature circulated, read in early A.A., and written by such notables as Glenn Clark, E. Stanley Jones, Charles Sheldon, Harry Emerson Fosdick, Norman Vincent Peale, Toyohiko Kagawa, and Samuel M. Shoemaker, plus innumerable writings by Oxford Group activists and admirers.

The Pot Hole As To Specific Contributors and Their Specific Ideas

A large body of resources, was pulled together by the work and thinking of two real alcoholics—Bill Wilson and Dr. Bob Smith. There was no basic text until 1939. There were no specific "steps" until 1939. There was not even a common agreement among the founders as to how much "God," "Jesus Christ," the "Bible," the Oxford Group, and Christian writings were to figure ultimately in the basic writings and approaches. The real definitive historical picture of A.A., from A.A.'s own standpoint, was to be found only in Bill Wilson's *Alcoholics Anonymous Comes of Age.* NY: Alcoholics Anonymous World Services, Inc., 1956; and in the later *Pass It On.* NY: Alcoholics Anonymous World Services, Inc., 1984; and *DR. BOB and the Good Oldtimers.* NY: Alcoholics Anonymous World Services, Inc., 1980. Even these historical works were not *completed* until the mid 1980's. And the interim period from 1935 to 1980 had seen the passing of both A.A. founders; the addition of a host of writings published by individual A.A. offices and areas; several solo efforts by Bill Wilson; and the emergence of leaders, writers, and thinkers such as Sister Ignatia, Father Ralph Pfau, Father Ed Dowling, S.J., Father John C. Ford, S.J., Richmond Walker, and A.A.'s own Ed Webster and Clarence Snyder—plus some new blood still in the wings..

Perhaps unaware of these varied roots and personalities, or opposed to their ideas, or protective of their "own" A.A. perspective, all too many programs and recovery books simply omit reference to the majority of present-day historical source materials and opt for some incomplete, simplified, and usually erroneous introductory material. They omit treasures that could and should make the program understandable. They omit historical facts that explain the Biblical and other recovery concepts. They add unusual words and ideas that confuse the facts. And they discard many of the original religious and scientific ideas and replace them with "universal," "secular," "spiritual but not religious," and "simple" approaches.

In over 17 years of research, writing, visiting, speaking, and comparing, I have seen a huge hole in each of the programs that have spun off from or out of Alcoholics Anonymous. They simply lack a concise, yet comprehensive, accurate, and informative segment or chapter on the spiritual history and roots of early Alcoholics Anonymous—a fellowship with astonishing success.

We'd fervently like to see all related programs and approaches include the simple matter in this guide. We believe this guide will preclude necessity for including the thousands of pages of ideas and materials that have helped define the whole. Instead, it will provide an outline, a workbook, a guidebook, and a resource. It can and should be usable as a preface, a chapter, a starting platform, a guiding approach, and an authoritative summary of just where it all came from, what it used to be like, how it can be described from an historical standpoint, and how it can supplement almost any and every recovery effort today.

Beef up your own program with the following scantily reported and often omitted sources of A.A. ideas—sources which, if learned and examined with care, might reveal many good reasons for today's shortfall in recoveries and results.

Summary of A.A.'s Basic Roots and Contributing Books, Persons, and Entities

The formative and developmental period for A.A. occurred from 1933 to the publication of its basic text and Twelve Steps in 1939. In that brief period, a small group of pioneers, primarily from Akron, took the Bible, their own experience with other sources, and personal contact with still-suffering alcoholics and developed a spiritual program of recovery with astonishing success rates of 75% and, by early 1940 in Cleveland, 93%. And all the recovered men and the few women in the fellowship boldly and positively asserting that they had been cured of alcoholism.

The kit of spiritual tools the Akron Pioneers used to get well were these:

The Bible (affectionately called "The Good Book")

Dr. Bob said A.A.'s basic ideas came from the Good Book and that the Book of James, Jesus' Sermon on the Mount, and 1 Corinthians 13 were absolutely essential to the solution of their problems. See Dick

14

B., *The Good Book and The Big Book: A.A.'s Roots in the Bible, 3rd ed.*, HI: Paradise Research Publications, Inc., 1938; *The James Club and The Original A.A. Program's Absolute Essentials.* HI: Paradise Research Publications, Inc. 2005; and *Why Early A.A. Succeeded.* HI: Paradise Research Publications, Inc., 2001.

The United Christian Endeavor Society

Dr. Bob said he had received excellent training in the Bible as a youngster—due not only to his family's frequent weekly attendance at North Congregational Church in St. Johnsbury, Vermont, but also due to his active participation in that church's Christian Endeavor Society. And Christian Endeavor's simple principles and practices consequently seem very much resemble to the Christian Fellowship program Dr. Bob and Bill W. developed, and Dr. Bob led in Akron. See Dick B., *James Club* and my website: http://dickb.com/Christian_Endeavor.shtml.

The Salvation Army

The original Salvation Army program focused on salvation, abstinence; redemption of the sinning criminals and alcoholics; helping them out of the slums and into new lives; and prodding them into helping others still stuck in the shadows. Its principles and practices influenced the mission where Bill and his "sponsor" Ebby began the march into what religion had to offer the alcoholic. The Salvation Army program much resembled the principal ingredients of the early Akron A.A. program (In certain locations, Salvation Army ARC programs still resemble the early A.A. look-a-like). See the series of lectures at Yale University in 1945, in which Bill Wilson himself addressed the clergy and scholars. Note should be taken of Lecture 26 by Rev. Francis W. McPeek, "The Role of Religious Bodies in the Treatment of Inebriety in the United States," *Twenty-nine Lectures with Discussions as Given at the Yale Summer School of Alcohol Studies.* New Haven: Quarterly Journal of Studies on Alcohol, 1945, pp. 414-415; Dick B*., The Salvation Army Factor*, on my website: http://www.dickb.com/index.shtml; Harold Begbie, *Twice Born Men.* NY: Fleming H. Revell, 1909; and the splendid discussion in Howard C. Clinebell, Ph.D. *Understanding and Counseling Persons with Alcohol, Drug, and Behavioral Addictions.* Rev. and Enl. ed.

Nashville: Abingdon Press, 1998. The importance of the Salvation Army to A.A. was underlined by a long dormant plan of Bill Wilson's to donate all royalty money from the Big Book over expenses to institutions like the Salvation Army "that would help alcoholics indirectly" (letter Henrietta Seiberling to John Seiberling Jr., dated October 23, 1945).

The Rescue or Gospel Missions

As he was presiding over a final review of A.A.'s basic textbook, Bill described how the Christian proponent John Henry Fitzhugh Mayo wanted to "retain" the Christian and Biblical materials which undergirded early A.A. successes. But Wilson commented on the need to expunge the "dogma we learned from the churches and the missions." And, of course, Bill owed a heavy, though seldom reported and recognized, debt to Calvary Rescue Mission operated by Rev. Sam Shoemaker's Calvary Episcopal Church. For it was there that Bill's sponsor Ebby, "got religion," and heeded the altar call, later to be baptized and become a communicant in Shoemaker's church. And it was there that Bill followed suit by going to the altar on another occasion, making a decision for Christ, and concluded that he had "for sure" been "born again." Bill got a taste of Bible, prayers, penitence, and surrender to Christ, in the mission itself. See Dick B., *The Conversion of Bill W.* HI: Paradise Research Publications, Inc., 2006.

Young Men's Christian Association

Both A.A.'s East Coast mentors—Oxford Group Founder Frank Buchman and Rev. Sam Shoemaker—were closely involved with the YMCA for several years. As to Buchman, see Mark O. Guldseth, *Streams.* Alaska: Fritz Creek Studios, 1982, pp. 84-85, 92-94, 128, Garth Lean, *Frank Buchman: A Life.* London: Constable, 1985, pp. 33-44, 81-82; and as to Buchman and Shoemaker, see Lean, *Buchman*, pp. 82, 108-131. Shoemaker's early materials were published by the Y's Association Press. Inspired by John R. Mott, the de facto leader of the world student Christian movement, both Buchman and Shoemaker espoused the YMCA's principles of personal work, evangelism, and Morning Watch. These foci all influenced A.A. development in the areas of one-on-one help, bringing people to Christ, and establishing the importance of morning meditation with Bible study, prayer,

16

guidance, and devotionals. See Dick B., *The Oxford Group and Alcoholics Anonymous: A Design for Living That Works.* HI: Paradise Research Publications, Inc.*; Pass It On,* p.130..

Dr. Frank Buchman's First Century Christian Fellowship—the Oxford Group

The twenty-eight Oxford Group ideas that impacted A.A. became incorporated in A.A. itself as a practical program of life-changing action. See Dick B., *Oxford Group and A.A.* A.A.'s own literature eventually acknowledged the debt. See *Pass It On,* where Bill Wilson is reported as writing: "I would give anything if you could avoid mentioning the matter [A.A.'s connection with the Oxford Group] at all, but it must be noted, I'm quite anxious to avoid words carrying criticism or sting. After all, we owe our lives to the group" (pp. 246-247)

The Rev. Samuel M. Shoemaker's Books, Teachings, and Personal Role

As an Oxford Group leader and an Episcopal rector, Shoemaker's personal relationship with Bill Wilson, and later A.A. itself, directly contributed most of the Oxford Group language and teachings that were codified into A.A.'s Big Book and Twelve Steps. See *The Language of the Heart,* p. 298; and Dick B., *Twelve Steps for You* and *New Light on Alcoholism: God, Sam Shoemaker, and A.A.,* 2d ed. HI: Paradise Research Publications, Inc., 1939.

Anne Ripley Smith, Wife of Dr. Bob, and "Mother of A.A."

In a journal she kept over the period from 1933 to 1939, Dr. Bob's wife Anne Smith wrote down in her own journal almost every one of the principles and practices of early A.A.—though the Big Book and Twelve Steps had not yet been written. Anne shared from this journal in morning quiet times and in meetings with early AAs and their families. And you can see that the principles of A.A. were articulated before the principles of A.A. were later articulated by Bill W. See Dick B., *Anne Smith's Journal: 1933-1939: A.A.'s Principles of Success.* In recognition of Anne's matchless role, Bill Wilson and many others called Anne the "Mother of A.A."

The Core Conversion Prescription from Dr. Carl Gustav Jung

It was the view of Dr. Carl Gustav Jung of Switzerland—passed along in Jung's conversations with Oxford Group member Rowland Hazard—that led Bill Wilson to believe that a transforming religious conversion experience was the spiritual ingredient required for victory over alcoholism. See *Bill W. My First Forty Years.* MN: Hazelden, 2000, pp. 123-139; *Pass It On*, pp. 381-386. A few AAs with practically no documentation have tried to debunk the idea that Rowland Hazard ever visited Dr. Carl Jung; but there are ample reasons to doubt their approach, particularly now that excellent studies have been done of the matter. See Cora Finch, *Stellar Fire: Carl Jung, a New England Family, and the Risks of Anecdote,* http://www.stellarfire.org., 2006. Wilson hailed Carl Jung as one of A.A.'s "founders" *Pass It On*, pp. 381, 383. And see Ron Ray, *The Forerunner–Rowland* (http://www.archivesinternational.org/AI/Documents/pdf/forerowland.pdf); and an extensive corroborative study by a scholar who did her thesis on the subject. See Amy Colwell Bluhm, Ph.D., "Veriticatio of C.G. Jung's analysis of Rowland Hazard and the history of Alcoholics Anonymous," *History of Psychology*, May, n.d.; American Psychological Assocation.

The Key Influence of Professor William James of Harvard

Both Bill Wilson and Dr. Bob studied William James' *The Varieties of Religious Experience*, from which Bill had concluded there was a validation of his own "hot flash" conversion experience. Little recognized too were the New Thought language and ideas that filtered into A.A. language via Rev. Sam Shoemaker's writings and those of others, including Anne Smith. Shoemaker particularly relied upon James' writings on self-surrender and conversion. See Samuel M. Shoemaker, Jr., *Realizing Religion.* NY: Association Press, 1929; William James, *The Varieties of Religious Experience.* NY: First Vintage Books/The Library of America Edition, 1990; and Dick B., *New Light on Alcoholism.*

The Ideas and Personal Influence of William Duncan Silkworth, M.D.

Most AAs seem inclined to believe that Silkworth's "Doctor's Opinion" in the front of their basic text shows Silkworth's direct influence on their First Step and the Big Book's discussions of alcoholism. However, recent findings establish a much greater Silkworth influence on the chain of events that led to A.A.'s earlier emphasis on Jesus Christ, the Great Physician.. See Dale Mitchel. *Silkworth: The Little Doctor Who Loved Drunks*. MN: Hazelden, 2002, pp. 42-51, 63, 66, 100, 104-109. Silkworth told Bill the rudiments of alcoholism, but Silkworth had a direct influence on Bill's seeking out the Great Physician, Jesus Christ, who, Silkworth said, could cure alcoholics. In addition to Mitchel's book, see: *Pass It On*; Dick B., *When Early AAs Were Cured and Why*; *The Conversion of Bill W.*; and Norman Vincent Peale, *The Positive Power of Jesus Christ.* Together these affirm Silkworth's frequent remarks that cure of alcoholism was available to one who gives his life to Jesus Christ.

The Christian Quiet Times or Quiet Hours and Devotionals

Quiet Time (with Bible study, prayer, seeking guidance, and reading Christian devotionals) was a "must" in early A.A. *DR. BOB and the Good Oldtimers*, p. 135. It affirmed, explained, and elaborated upon the Biblical ideas then being studied; and it heavily influenced A.A.'s Eleventh Step. See Dick B., *Good Morning: Quiet Time, Morning Watch, Meditation, and Early A.A.*, 2d ed. HI: Paradise Research Publications, Inc., 1998.; *The Akron Genesis of Alcoholics Anonymous*, 2d ed. HI: Paradise Research Publications, Inc., 1998; and *The Books Early AAs Read for Spiritual Growth*, 7th ed.; Rev. Sam Shoemaker was a particularly strong advocate of Quiet Time and spelled out the ingredients of quiet, prayer, Bible study, listening to God, and the reading of Christian literature. See Dick B., *New Light on Alcoholism: God, Sam Shoemaker, and A.A..*, 2d ed., HI: Paradise Research Publications, Inc., 1991.

Non-Oxford Group Literature by leading Christian Writers

Explanations of Bible segments, quiet times, prayer, and healing were circulated among A.A. pioneers from the writings of Henry Drummond, Oswald Chambers, E. Stanley Jones, Harry Emerson Fosdick, and many others. See Dick B., *The Books Early AAs Read*; *Dr. Bob and His Library*, 3rd ed.; HI: Paradise Research Publications,

Inc., 1998; *Anne Smith's Journal; Making Known the Biblical History and Roots of Alcoholics Anonymous.*

Lay Recovery Ideas of Richard Peabody

Richard Peabody wrote *The Common Sense of Drinking*—read by both Bill W. and Dr. Bob. Though Peabody was merely a lay therapist and though he ultimately died drunk, a number of specific phrases almost directly attributable to *The Common Sense of Drinking*, can be found in Wilson's Big Book—phrases speaking of no cure for alcoholism, half measures availed nothing, once-an-alcoholic-always-an-alcoholic. Richard R. Peabody, *The Common Sense of Drinking*. Atlantic Monthly Press Book, 1939. Dick B., *When Early AAs Were Cured and Why*, 3rd ed., HI: Paradise Research Publications, Inc, 2006; *Cured: Proven Help for Alcoholics* and Addicts. 2d ed. HI: Paradise Research Publications, Inc., 2006; and Mel B., *New Wine: The Spiritual Roots of the Twelve Step Miracle.* MN: Hazelden Foundation, 1991.

New Thought Writings of Emmet Fox, Mary Baker Eddy, Unity and Others

New Thought writers were read by AAs, and some of their language and concepts can be found embedded in A.A.'s later language—even though their writings did not espouse and actually rejected the born-again Christianity of early A.A. See Dick B., *Making Known The Biblical History and Roots of Alcoholics Anonymous.* 3rd ed,, 2006; *The Books Early AAs Read for Spiritual Growth.* 7th ed., 1998; *Dr. Bob and His* Library, 3rd ed., 1998.; and Mel B. *New Wine.*

The Hands-on Personal Work of Recovered Alcoholics with Newcomers

Pioneer AAs plunged into one-on-one work with other, new or wet alcoholics. In so doing, they applied the foregoing ideas, hospitalized drunks, concentrated on the Bible, prayer, and devotional literature, and added some Oxford Group practices for changing lives. This emphasis is best shown in books about Clarence Snyder (Dick B., *That Amazing Grace*; Three Clarence Snyder Old-timer Sponsees, *Our A.A. Faith-Based Legacy*; and Mitch K. *How It Worked: The Story of Clarence H. Snyder.* The expression "flying blind period" is a

20

misnomer. You don't fly blind with God. But you can and do use His tools to bring healings and cures to others if you apply the A.A. principles of love and service. Articulation of service through fellowship and witness was picked up from the Oxford Group and its life-changing techniques. See Harold Begbie, *Life-Changers*. NY: G. P. Putnam's Sons, 1927; Dick B., *The Oxford Group and Alcoholics Anonymous;* Jerry G. Dunn. *God is For the Alcoholic*. Chicago: The Moody Bible Institute of Chicago, 1965.

3.

The Two, Diverse Recovery Program Origins; and the Three Emerging, Varied, Approaches in Akron, Cleveland, and New York

United Christian Endeavor and Dr. Bob's Youth

One of the two, diverse A.A. recovery programs quite clearly centered around Dr. Bob, what he did as a youngster, and what he led in Akron from 1935 to 1939.

The early A.A. program of the Akron pioneers really began with the training Dr. Bob had received as a youngster in attending about four church service and prayer meetings each week at the North Congregational Church in St. Johnsbury, Vermont. The training seeded the program of the United Christian Endeavor Society of the young people in that church. And the Christian Endeavor Society's actual practices consisted of confession of Christ, Bible Study, Prayer meetings, Conversion meetings, reading and discussion of religious literature, Quiet Hour, fellowship and witness. Christian Endeavor emphasized love and service. It was self-governing and self-supporting—just as early A.A. was originally intended to be.

Years later, in Akron, after having been apprised of Russell Firestone's seemingly miraculous deliverance from alcoholism, Dr. Bob was brought into a tiny Oxford Group meeting consisting of a few Groupers and a few alcoholics and their families. It was in that fellowship that Dr. Bob began to make changes in his life in hope or at least the hope of his wife and the group that he would be able to stop drinking just as Russell Firestone had done. Bob went all out for the practices and back to the religious training he'd had as a youngster. He read the Bible from cover to cover three times. He joined a new

23

church. He read everything he could find on the Oxford Group, as well as an immense amount of other religious literature. At the meetings and in his own life, there was Bible study, prayer, seeking of God's strength and guidance, and fellowship. But Dr. Bob did not want to quit drinking, and he didn't. Finally, at a meeting convened by Henrietta Seiberling of the rubber clan, the group got Dr. Bob to admit to his alcoholism, asked him to join them in prayer, and—as a group—prayed for Bobs deliverance from alcoholism. But Bob did not quit drinking—not, that is, until in apparent answer to the prayers, Bill Wilson appeared in Akron out of New York, was seeking out another drunk to help, was put in touch with Henrietta Seiberling, was regarded by her as "manna from heaven" in answer to prayers, and in turn introduced to Dr. Bob at the Gate Lodge home of Henrietta and her three children. See Dick B. *Henrietta B. Seiberling: Ohio's Lady with a Cause,* 2d ed. HI: Paradise Research Publications, Inc., 2005.

Developments in New York Centered on Shoemaker and the Oxford Group

The second of A.A.'s two diverse roots centered around Bill Wilson and the long chain of events, people, and entities that led from Switzerland to New York.

The origin and development of the New York group was entirely different. Its roots began with the visits of Rowland Hazard to Dr. Carl Jung in Switzerland and Jung's diagnosis of Hazard's "chronic mind of an alcoholic" likely to be cured only by a conversion experience. This Rowland sought in the Oxford Group, A First Century Christian Fellowship, founded by Lutheran Minister Frank Buchman. Essentially, the Oxford Group sought to change lives by putting its new people through a practical program of action. Their basic formula for procedure was: Sin is the problem. Christ is the cure. The result is a miracle." (Mark O. Guldseth, *Streams*. Alaska: Fritz Creek Studios, 1945) As I discovered and publicized in my title *The Oxford Group and Alcoholics Anonymous*, Buchman's life-changing program embraced some twenty-eight principles that were to impact on A.A. They were learned by Rowland Hazard. They were taught by Rowland and others to Ebby Thacher, a seemingly hopeless drunk. Rowland and some Oxford Group friends lodged Thacher in Calvary Mission in

New York, and Thacher there "got religion," was converted, and sought out his old school-mate and alcoholic friend, Bill Wilson. Thacher convinced young Bill that God had done for him, in relieving him of alcoholism, what he could not do for himself; and Bill, in turn, went to Calvary Mission, made a decision for Christ, and checked into Towns Hospital for the fourth time for treatment of his alcoholism. There Thacher indoctrinated Wilson further in Oxford Group principles; and Wilson himself surrendered his life to God. Wilson had what Bill believed was a conversion experience, with the result that Bill not only never drank again, but also believed he had found a cure for alcoholism that could benefit countless others. Bill set out to change lives in Towns Hospital, in Calvary Mission, and in Oxford Group meetings. But Bill had no success whatever. And it was after five months of failed evangelism that Bill went to Akron on a business deal—there confronted with the choice of resuming his drinking or finding another drunk to help.

The First Meeting of Alcoholics Bill W. and Dr. Bob

Though reluctant to come, Dr. Bob was persuaded by Henrietta Seiberling and by his own wife and son to meet with Bill—planning to stay a mere 15 minutes. But the talk lasted almost six hours at Henrietta's home. The two men hit it off. Bill thought he had carried a powerful message to Bob. And Bob said he had heard it all before but was impressed with Bill's idea of service and his unselfish efforts with Bob. Whereupon the two began discussing the Bible and Oxford Group principles to the end of figuring how they might help others. Bill moved into the Smith home in Akron for three months. Bob went on one last bender that summer; but on June 10, 1935, he had his last drink, and A.A. was founded. This was, in turn, followed almost immediately by the success of the two men in leading A.A. Number Three (Bill Dotson) to a cure; and this third success marked the founding of Akron Group Number One—the first A.A. group. Bill, Bob, Bob's wife Anne, Henrietta Seiberling, and the small group of Oxford Group helpers continued as a fellowship throughout the summer of 1935. Then Bill Wilson returned to New York with the basic ideas in place. There were no Steps. There were no Traditions. There was no basic text. There were the Bible, the Christian devotionals and literature they studied, and some Oxford Group principles they applied. There were no drunkalogs. Even their stories were considered unimportant and of minimal value. But for the next two-and-a-half years from the summer of 1935 to the early part of 1938, the Akron program developed with astonishing results. It was soon called a Christian Fellowship—with its alcoholic squad reaching out; one meeting a week as a so-called clandestine lodge of the Oxford Group; daily Bible study, prayer, Quiet Time, use of devotionals, reading of Christian literature, conversion meetings, virtual half-way houses for the newcomers primarily in the Smith home, and short hospitalization of newcomers where they were daily visited by Dr. Bob and Akron members who had recovered.

The Simple Program of the Akron Christian Fellowship

The Akron program closely resembled the practices in Christian Endeavor that Dr. Bob learned as a youngster. There was also an incorporation of long-standing Salvation Army principles such as abstinence, bringing new people to Christ and salvation, extending shelter and food to newcomers, engaging in prayer and Bible study, and encouraging participants to seek out others to help with the message of salvation and deliverance from alcoholism. Medical aspects and hospitalization appear to have come from Dr. Bob's own experience as a practicing physician and the information Bill had learned in Towns Hospital and from his psychiatrist Dr. Silkworth. Dr. Bob's wife gathered the details of their work together from 1933 to 1939 in a spiritual journal she wrote and shared with others at meetings, in daily Quiet Times she led in the mornings, and in personal talks. All types of Christian literature—devotionals, Oxford Group and Shoemaker writings, and the writings of well-known authors like Fosdick, Drummond, E. Stanley Jones, Glenn Clark, Kagawa, and a host of other leaders of the day—were circulated among the AAs and their families. There appears to have been little or no attempt to achieve the "conversion" experience solution which had so dominated Bill Wilson's thinking on the East Coast and which had in fact produced few if any successes.

The Akron program was considered so successful, among the forty pioneers (previously considered medically incurable) who really tried, that Bill Wilson sought funds from John D. Rockefeller, Jr. to pay the bills and move the message forward. Rockefeller dispatched his agent Frank Amos to Akron for a thorough investigation. Amos reported back to Rockefeller that the program was much like that of the gospel of the First Century Christians, was led by Dr. Bob, was indeed miraculous, and consisted of seven points which Amos described in the following words which we here *again* repeat from the points made above:

- An alcoholic must realize that he is an alcoholic, incurable from a medical viewpoint, and that he must never drink anything with alcohol in it.
- He must surrender himself absolutely to God, realizing that in himself there is no hope.
- Not only must he want to stop drinking permanently, he must remove from his life other sins such as hatred, adultery, and others which frequently accompany alcoholism. Unless he will do this absolutely, Smith and his associates refuse to work with him.
- He must have devotions every morning–a "quiet time" of prayer and some reading from the Bible and other religious literature. Unless this is faithfully followed, there is grave danger of backsliding.
- He must be willing to help other alcoholics get straightened out. This throws up a protective barrier and strengthens his own willpower and convictions.
- It is important, but not vital, that he meet frequently with other reformed alcoholics and form both a social and a religious comradeship.
- Important, but not vital, that he attend some religious service at least once weekly.

4.

Parallels from the Groups Contributing to Akron's Pioneer Program

Christian Endeavor Society Parallels

The Christian Endeavor Societies of Dr. Bob's youth focused on these practices: Confession of Jesus Christ; Bible study; prayer meetings; conversion meetings; reading of religious literature; Quiet Hour; love and service. They were self-supporting, self-governing, and supported their particular local church. Except for abstinence and helping drunks, early A.A. resembles them all.

Salvation Army Parallels

The original Salvation Army practices might be, and have been, summarized as advocating abstinence, confession of Christ, focus on Bible and prayer, elimination of sin, and helping others, not yet saved and restored, to whole lives. Early A.A. used them all.

Oxford Group Parallels

Reduced to their essence, the twenty-eight Oxford Group life-changing ideas meant a belief in the Creator; surrender to Him and doing His will; elimination of sin by applying the art of the 5 C's—Confidence, Confession, Conviction, Conversion, and Continuance; living by the Four Absolute Standards of Jesus Christ—honesty, purity, unselfishness and love; making restitution for harms done; Quiet Time with Bible study, prayer, and seeking of guidance; fellowship, and witness—changing the lives of others by the same techniques. Wilson used them all.

Gospel and Rescue Mission Parallels

Focusing on then altar call and acceptance of Christ, the Mission technique did resemble early A.A. surrenders. So too its emphasis on Bible reading and prayer. Even the provision of food, shelter, and support were also A.A. hallmarks—points to be remembered when some inexperienced AA tells a newcomer that he or she merely needs to follow the dictum: "Don't drink, and go to meetings." I know of no evidence that such a technique ever worked—in early A.A. or its predecessors. In a little noticed remark about the writing of the Big Book, Bill pointed out that A.A.'s southern friend fits M., "wanted a fairly religious book infused with some of the dogma we had picked up from the churches and missions which had tried to help us." (Bill W., "Where did the 12 Steps come from?" July 1953 *A.A. Grapevine*).

YMCA Parallels

Like all the foregoing but the Missions, the YMCA emphasized Quiet Time, and the concomitant Bible study and prayer. Religious comradeship and the acquisition of skills for better living were two aspects resembling pioneer A.A. work. But the "salvation" emphasis of other Christian movements did not appear to be a force from the YMCA.

A New and Different Look at The Akron Program as Reported to Rockefeller by Frank Amos

Rockefeller's agent, Frank Amos, thoroughly investigated the early program, reported its successes, and pointed to Dr. Bob as the leader. Amos declared the program had seven simple elements—the first five mandatory and the last two simply recommended: The elements he found, can be summarized as abstinence; establishing a child-of-God relationship with the Creator; absolute reliance on the Creator; elimination of sinful conduct, daily fellowship with the Creator through continuing obedience, Bible study, prayer, and seeking guidance; helping other alcoholics get well; engaging in religious and social comradeship; and attending church. See above for the precise words Amos used to describe Akron's simple program.

Dr. Silkworth's Concise Summary of Parallel Elements

Writing about the program on July 27, 1939, shortly after the Big Book was published, Dr. William D. Silkworth (who had treated Bill Wilson, seen Bill's recovery, and watched the movement grow) said, "The essential features of this new approach, without psychological embellishment, are:" (1) One alcoholic can secure the confidence of another. (2) He cites his own case and medical opinion that there may be no hope for him save a spiritual experience. (3) The patient has a serious dilemma—to have a spiritual experience or be destroyed by alcohol. (4) He believes he can't be untangled by human means; he is persuaded by the recovered alcoholic's peculiar ability; "he turns to religion with an entire willingness and accepts without reservation a serious religious proposal and then is able to acquire a set of religious beliefs and undergo the change common to religious experience;" (5) He is advised to "do certain things which are obviously good psychology, good morals and good religion": (a) Make a moral appraisal of himself and disclose the findings to another he trusts. (b) Adjust bad personal relationships, setting right, so far as possible, his wrongs of the past. (c) "Recommit himself daily, or hourly if need be, to God's care and direction, asking for strength." (d) If possible, attend weekly fellowship meetings and actively lend a hand with alcoholic newcomers. See Mitchel, *Silkworth,* pp. 158-161. Does that sound like the Akron program and some of its predecessors?

Shoemaker's Brief Explanation to AAs themselves of a "Religious Experience," "Spiritual Experience" or "Spiritual Awakening" as these were variously called

At A.A.'s 20th Anniversary and International Convention at St. Louis, Missouri, in 1955, Sam Shoemaker—who was invited to speak to the entire assembly—spelled out what he believed were four universal factors in all genuine "spiritual awakenings."

These four factors contain a remarkably simple, composite, parallel road to the spiritual solution in the other organizations we've mentioned. In my title *New Light on Alcoholism*, p. 330, and in the body of Bill's *Alcoholics Anonymous Comes of Age*, pp. 261-270, the four key elements are listed as:

(1) Prayer.

(2) Conversion.

(3) Fellowship.

(4) Witness.

The Common Thread

Note the similar elements drawn from, and discussed by, the programs and people who were instrumental in defining all these roots. Note also the simplicity of the elements—with variances only due to the institution, the professional status, and the religion involved. They appear, as a group, to provide a reliable common thread for spiritual recovery that relies on God:

1. A willingness, stemming from the inadequacy of medical and human help and from the successful experience of another of the same feather, to accept without reservation a religious approach and solution—that God is, and rewards those who diligently seek Him (See Hebrews 11:6).

2. A commitment to complete, permanent, abstinence, and resisting temptation.

3. Accepting Christ as the way to establishing a relationship with the Creator and becoming one of His children; with the afflicted then entrusting himself or herself to God's care and direction, and asking for strength.

4. Eliminating sinful conduct using the process of making a moral appraisal, confessing sins, rectifying relationships, and righting wrongs of the past.

5. Growing in fellowship with God through Bible study, prayer, seeking revelation, and obeying His will—loving God and your neighbor with all your heart, soul, mind, and strength.

6. Fellowshipping with like-minded believers and, as well, loving, witnessing, and lending a hand to newcomers and bringing them to salvation, sobriety, spiritual wholeness, and service to others.

5.

Jerry Dunn's Relevant Viewpoints

An elaboration of the process by an experienced, religious, churched, A.A. Old Timer who applied the principles to the many alcoholics and addicts he helped.

I include the following from Jerry Dunn's book for several reasons. Long ago, his book was handed to me by a Christian Bookstore Minister, and without comment. I read it at the time and figured it would not be useful in the modern-day A.A. scene which finds so many throwing rocks at religion, church, and the Bible. Then I was asked to speak at the first international convention of Alcoholics Victorious; and Jerry and I were the two principal speakers. As I listened to his story, I realized he'd been round the track many times— drinking, debauchery, arrest, jail, finding Christ, tackling A.A., becoming a lay minister, supervising a treatment program, and continuously serving others. Then, for this present title, I read Jerry again. I saw that, as a seasoned veteran, he had long combined so many of the common elements of successful programs, belonged to A.A., and placed his foot on the ladder that led to heaven. His material, as summarized, can perhaps help you to see how a simple chunk of historical material can be packaged, marketed, and used today to help the many who are floundering in the road between 12 Step movements and religious movements. As a matter of fact, that is the basic approach of Alcoholics Victorious which is a harbor for many who want to accept Christ and some who are still suffering in regular 12 Step programs. Interestingly, Alcoholics Victorious is a recent acquisition by the Association of Gospel Rescue Missions, and therefore has the further enlightenment and support that comes from that environment.

In his title *God Is For The Alcoholic* (a book that sold over half a million copies), Jerry G. Dunn asserted that God has provided the following "way of escape" for the alcoholic at his bottom (See Jerry Dunn, *God Is For The Alcoholic*. Chicago: Moody Press, 1965, p. 55):

Simple Help for The Still-Suffering Individual

1. Encourage him in his desire to stop.

2. Help him to face his problem.

3. Provide him with medical care, so that he can have the help modern medicine can give him. See that he gets a complete physical checkup.

4. Help him to understand that he can't overcome alcohol addiction by himself.

5. Introduce him to the power of God.

6. Teach him to keep in daily touch with God's power.

Five Ways To Help The Alcoholic

Standing on the platform of complete abstinence, Dunn then suggested **five ways to help the alcoholic**. And, as you look at the Dunn's five ways—expressed in detail as follows, just picture what Dr. Bob and the early AAs were doing in their days of confessing Christ, studying the Bible, holding prayer meetings, asking for guidance, and then turning to help the newcomer alcoholic. Jerry's five ways are as follows.

This first way, Dunn said, "**is to pray for him**." He quotes an S.D. Gordon book owned by Dr. Bob: "but you can't do more than pray until you have prayed." Then the ground rules to be followed: (1) Be sure you are a member of God's family—prayer is the privilege and duty of the children of God. (2) Stand on God's promise to answer prayer. (3) Make the right approach through private prayer after examining yourself, confessing the sin in your life, and asking God to blot it out; (4) Make the right approach through public prayer—where a group of Christians share mutual burdens and pray together for a given problem or a certain situation; (5) Make use of intercessory prayer lifting the alcoholic into the hands of the Lord and petitioning God to deliver him; (6) Crying out to God; making sure to ask; expecting an answer; and praying for men in authority (Dunn, *God*, pp. 82-96).

The second way "**is to present the gospel to him at the earliest possible moment**." Dunn tells of his associate Garland Thompson who had never been an alcoholic, nor made a special study of alcoholism, but devoted his entire life to prayer and personal witnessing. Men who were won to Christ said gratefully, "Know what set me to thinking? It was Garland Thompson putting his arm around me and telling me that God loves me and, because He loves me, you guys here at the Mission were going to help me. I was pretty drunk, but that got through to me." We must point up to the alcoholic (who is making a profession of faith) that faith in Christ means a new life: "Therefore if any man be in Christ, he is a new creature; old things are passed away; behold, old things are become new" II Corinthians 5:17 (Dunn, *God*, pp. 98-105).

The third way "**is to offer fellowship—communion, intimacy, joint interest, and feeling**." "Alcoholics Anonymous, the most successful organization involved in the treatment of the alcoholic, has made fellowship a cornerstone in their efforts to help the individual. We must do the same. . . We can have rapport with the alcoholic because we have been separated from God by sin just as he has been separated from God by sin. And we have been delivered, by Christ, from our sin, even as he can be delivered, by Christ, from his sin." Dunn cites Luke 5:31-32, quoting Jesus: "I came not to call the righteous, but sinners to repentance." Then he cites 1 Timothy 2:4 to establish God's will that *all* men be saved and come to a knowledge of the truth. "How can we help an alcoholic," Dunn asked? Dunn's answer as to fellowship: "By creating around him an atmosphere that would create in him a desire to help, One of the most effective ways of doing this is to offer him fellowship in the name of our loving Lord." (Dunn, *God*, pp. 106-126)

The fourth way **is to "show Christ's long-suffering to us as a pattern for others to follow in their treatment of sinners**." As Dunn put it, "The patience of Job would have been sorely tried by an alcoholic." "But God saved me and delivered me and my family. He can do the same for any individual—even the degenerate filthy alcoholic addict—who calls upon His name." (Dunn, *God*, pp.127-138).

The fifth way **is to "Let the alcoholic stand on his own two feet."** "If we sin, we should be rebuked. If we repent, we ought to be forgiven." Firmness is the key, said Jerry. (Dunn, *God*, pp. 139-152).

Five Ways That The Alcoholic Can Help Himself

Dunn moves on with how you can help the alcoholic to the critical responsibility the alcoholic has for helping himself. Dunn discusses **five ways that the alcoholic can help himself** (Dunn, *God*, pp. 155-202):

Transfer his dependency to God.

Talk with God daily.

Share himself.

Live a step at a time: "God knows the end from the beginning. He will direct our paths if we ask Him to. We can only follow God's instructions one day at a time (Matthew 6:34)—the origin of "Easy Does It" and "One Day at a Time."

Keep a perpetual inventory. "I have found that my inventory has helped me to say no to temptations. I say when a particular temptation confronts me, 'That's out of my old life. It is not a part of my new life. I'm not going to do that thing."

6.

Picking Your Way Along Today

Taking Up the Common Thread; Learning What Others Did; Using It Today

You can invent a self-made religion. You can invoke half-baked prayers. You can rely on idolatrous powers such as chairs, radiators, and doorknobs. You can say that you prefer one religious denomination over another. You can decline to read religious literature, to hang out with like-minded believers, and to attend a church or religious group of your own choosing. But you cannot escape the commonality in the foregoing unique and effective religious ideas for curing alcoholism.

Dr. Bob laid the religious solution on the line for newcomers. He asked them point-blank if they believed in God. He addressed the readers of the Big Book by stating he felt sorry for them if they were atheists, agnostics, or skeptics. "Your Heavenly Father," Bob wrote," will never let you down." See *DR. BOB and the Good Oldtimers*, p. 144; and *Alcoholics Anonymous*, 4th ed, p. 181.

Though declaring that he had formerly been an atheist, Bill Wilson opted for Sam Shoemaker's approach that he needed to find God; he needed a vital religious experience; and he needed Jesus Christ. See Samuel Shoemaker, *Realizing Religion*, pp. 1-9. And though Bill removed from his Big Book drafts all references to Shoemaker, to the Bible, to the need for Christ, and to a conversion experience, Wilson explicitly fashioned a program to "find God" and "establish a relationship with God." Even Bill's qualifying phrase "God as we understood Him" was no different from the identical expression long used by Rev. Sam Shoemaker in such books as *Children of the Second*

Birth—where, talking about becoming children of Yahweh, the Creator—Sam just told them to surrender to as much of Him as they understood when they gave their lives over to His care and direction. Then, in his Big Book, Bill pressed the Biblical point: There is a God. Bill invoked and virtually quoted verbatim Shoemaker's own challenge that God either is or He isn't. And concluded that if you followed certain Steps, you'd find or rediscover God, have a conversion experience, be changed, and stay sober because [It] "was a form of lunacy which only God Almighty could cure," Bill said. See Dick B. *Akron Genesis*, p. 13. And Bill also declared in the Big Book: "Even so has God restored us all to our right minds. . . He has come to all who have honestly sought Him. When we drew near to Him, He disclosed Himself to us!" (*Alcoholics Anonymous*, 1ˢᵗ ed., 1939, p. 69).

Note the new and different direction and the departure from the Akron roots that Bill took as he began discussing and fashioning his 1939 Big Book and 12 Steps

By a bare majority vote in A.A.'s original tiny fellowship, Bill was authorized to write a basic text; and most of those voting undoubtedly believed the new book would be a report on the elements of the Akron Program—they even proposed calling the new effort "The James Club."

But Bill had other ideas. He wanted commercial sales of the books. He formed a corporation—Works Publishing Company. He prepared a prospectus and sold shares of stock. He was importuned by his partner Hank Parkhurst to avoid describing a religious program. He did discuss the manuscript with, and took extensive advice from, his friend Rev. Samuel M. Shoemaker—even asking Sam to write the Twelve Steps, but Sam declined. Bill was determined to placate the atheists and agnostics, few though they were. And all overt references, in his manuscript, to the early Christian Fellowship, the Bible, its Bible study and prayer meetings, Jesus Christ, and the religious literature they studied were removed. Some 400 to 800 pages were tossed out. (See *Pass It On.*, p. 204). Hazelden historian Bill Pittman personally told me that Bill Wilson's secretary Ruth Hock had informed him (Pittman) that the trashed material was mostly Christian in tone and content. And Bill's wife Lois Wilson seemed to corroborate the point when she remembered, "Finally it was agreed that the book should present a

40

universal spiritual program, not a specific religious one, since all drunks were not Christian." See *Lois Remembers*, p. 113.

Bill seemingly adopted the Oxford Group simple life-changing program of action to "find God" and "change lives." But Bill also included a host of new elements that did not resemble the common elements as outlined above and as originally taken from such sources as Christian Endeavor, the Salvation Army, Silkworth, and the Bible, to the extent described above.

Here's What Bill Tenderly Did with the Original Sources—Akron and the other ideas above.

Carl Jung and William James Ideas as Modified

From Dr. Carl Jung, Bill offered the solution—a conversion experience. But he changed that religious conversion phrase to one used by William James and Sam Shoemaker—a religious experience. Then he opted for the phrase "spiritual experience"—a term used in the Oxford Group. And Bill adopted the thesis of Professor William James that people could be cured by valid religious experiences.

The Oxford Group Link Through Rowland Hazard as Adapted

Rowland Hazard had learned the conversion solution from Jung; and, upon Jung's suggestion, had aligned himself with a religious group— the Oxford Group—founded by Dr. Frank Buchman. There appears to be no evidence that Rowland had a "conversion experience," but it seems clear that Rowland learned Buchman's Oxford Group precepts, passed them along to Ebby Thacher, who (with Rowland and others) convinced Bill that the Oxford Group life-changing ideas would produce the needed conversion and, as they were thought to have done with Rowland, producing the cure for alcoholism as well. For the Oxford Group slogan was "Sin is the problem. Christ is the cure. The result is a miracle." (See Mark O. Guldseth, *Streams*. Alaska: Fritz Creek Studios, 1945, p.144)

The Views and Efforts of Silkworth as Re-worked

Discarding all of the mention by Dr. Silkworth himself of Jesus Christ, the Great Physician, and the power of Jesus Christ as the solution, Wilson simply incorporated Silkworth's remarks on the problem—alcoholism was said thereby to be an obsession of the mind coupled with an allergy of the body that would, if not arrested, get progressively worse and eventually lead to death, brain damage, or jail.

The Special Place of Co-founder Sam Shoemaker

You cannot read the language of Bill's Big Book and Twelve Steps without encountering the words and phrases of Bill's friend Rev. Sam Shoemaker. You can find the details and parallels in Dick B., *Twelve Steps for You. 4ᵗ ed.* HI: Paradise Research Publications, Inc., 2005; *The James Club and the Original A.A. Program's Absolute Essentials, 4ᵗʰ ed.* HI: Paradise Research Publications, Inc., 2005; and *Our A.A. Legacy to the Faith Community.* FL: Came To Believe Publications, 2005. And Shoemaker himself drew on ideas and language used by Carl Jung, William James, Oxford Group writers, and Dr. Silkworth.

The Side-line Roles of Richard Peabody and New Thought Writers

There is good reason to believe—just from examining the words and phrases themselves—that Bill interjected into the Big Book and Steps ideas from lay-therapist Peabody and such New Thought writers as Henry Drummond, Mary Baker Eddy, the Fillmores, Ralph Waldo Trine, Emmet Fox, and others. Such phrases as once-an-alcoholic-always-an-alcoholic, no-cure-for-alcoholism, and half-measures availed us nothing seem directly extracted from Peabody's Common Sense of Drinking. Similarly the strange expression "higher power" and such words as cosmic consciousness, fourth dimension, Universal Mind, and the like have a strange ring when compared to the Bible and the Bible roots of A.A. But they do represent ideas that were floating in the minds and literature read by some of the pioneers.

The Discernable Roots in Twelve Step Language

There have been many attempts to correlate the Twelve Steps with various Bible verses, with various Oxford Group ideas, with New Thought language, and other sources. But the simple fact is that the Twelve Steps came from the many sources mentioned above. And my title *Twelve Steps for You* takes each of the Twelve Steps and examines it in terms of each of the sources and ideas the contributed to it. Almost all unable to be reconciled with today's typical fellowship meetings and talk.

The work should be immensely helpful in studying, understanding, taking, teaching, and practicing the Steps of any Twelve Step or similar spin-off program or fellowship.

The Further Additions and Amendments from 1940 to 1955

I see no profit here in describing with particularity the history, changes, and ingredients of the A.A. program after the First Edition of the Big Book was published in 1939. The reason is that the pre-1939 program is the one that has been forgotten, that has been shelved, and yet still stands as the original program that produced extraordinary results not since achieved. But it *is* important to note that the changes—after the changed approach by Wilson in 1939—were themselves many in number and form. And to state that they materially affected the shape and language of the A.A. fellowship today.

Clarence Snyder

Breaking off from Akron Number One in the interest of assuring that Roman Catholics would be welcome in A.A., Clarence Snyder organized the first meeting of Alcoholics Anonymous in Cleveland in May, 1939. He took with him the principles of the Bible, the Four Absolutes of the Oxford Group, the Big Book, and the Twelve Steps. Clarence was, perhaps, an important beacon light as to what A.A. could be if it remembered and applied its roots. And the Cleveland groups soared from one to thirty in a year and achieved a documented 93% success rate. Clarence authored pamphlets on how to take the 12

Steps and on Sponsorship. *Cleveland Central Bulletins* quoted the Bible and the Oxford Group's Four Absolutes. And pulling in and indoctrinating newcomers was first in priority.

Sister Ignatia and St. Thomas Hospital

Shortly after the 1939 developments, Sister Ignatia began working with Dr. Bob directly and admitting alcoholics to St. Thomas Hospital in Akron where she and Bob treated some 5,000 alcoholics. Sister Ignatia worked in harmony with Dr. Bob, consulted Anne Smith often, and yet introduced ideas of her own—still holding to the importance of initial hospitalization just as A.A. in Akron had done. The good Sister passed out Thomas a Kempis's *The Imitation of Christ,* wrote materials on treatment, and seems to have originated the idea of giving out medallions on graduation from the alcoholic ward. She earned immense popularity in the Mid-west.

Richmond Walker

Having cut his teeth in the Oxford Group, Richmond Walker went on to write several popular books such as *For Drunks Only.* MN: Hazelden, n.d.—laying out the principles of the program as he saw them. And he ultimately wrote the materials that became the presently popular *Twenty-Four Hour Book,* still published by Hazelden. This book is widely used in treatment programs and widely read by AAs even today. It completely altered the nature of the original Quiet Time practices in Akron.

Father Ed Dowling, S.J.

In 1940, the Jesuit priest, Father Ed Dowling, S.J., became the friend, confidant, and "spiritual sponsor" of Bill Wilson. Dowling was one of the two men (Father John Ford, S.J., being the other) who edited in the 1950's two new books Bill Wilson wrote—*Alcoholics Anonymous Comes of Age* and *Twelve Steps and Twelve Traditions* NY: Alcoholics Anonymous World Services, Inc, 1987. Dowling and Wilson communicated frequently. At Bill's invitation, Dowling addressed AAs at their Twentieth Anniversary Convention in St. Louis. The extent of his impact on A.A. itself seems still to be evaluated.

Father Ralph Pfau

Father Pfau, also a Roman Catholic priest, developed a following of his own, particularly in the Midwest—writing two major books and a host of pamphlets on sobriety. The latter were called the "Golden Books" and are still in wide circulation in Mid-west A.A. They appear to be particularly popular with Roman Catholic AAs in that area, although Professor Glenn Chesnut, who has written extensively on Pfau, wrote me that Pfau's works were popular in many A.A. areas around the United States, and not just among Roman Catholics.

Ed Webster and the Regional Factors and Literature

Bill Wilson became severely depressed in the period spanning 1942 to 1955. Such depressions had begun in his youth when his parents separated, when his first love died unexpectedly, and on other occasions. Bill's Secretary Nell Wing told me that this was a "terrible period" for A.A. However, the 1942 to 1955 period marked the period when many non-Wilson, non-New York materials were published by local offices; and in the vacuum of Bill's active leadership, a good many regional publications sprang up. These were widely used in Minnesota, Washington, D.C., and the State of Washington for many years. At least one became the forerunner of a work within A.A. today called "back to basics"—the "basics" being those developed in the 1940's and quite different from the Akron basics.

The Turn-about from 1950 to 1955 following deaths of Anne and Dr. Bob

As the foregoing elements began to be added in the 1940's, Bill's disabilities from depression were in full swing. And Dr. Bob was growing older and infirm while Anne Smith was losing her sight. At the end of the decade, the Smiths were dead; Wilson was still depressed; and new factors involving "traditions," "concepts," "warranties," and organizational structures were becoming a norm, at least in New York. Finally, the Second Edition of the Big Book was published; and it not only removed some of the original Big Book stories, but also changed the basic solution from a "spiritual experience" to a "spiritual awakening." It manufactured and placed new "personality change" language in an appendix to A.A.'s basic text. This to explain why people didn't need to have the hot flash experience upon which Bill founded his whole Big Book approach. Even the confusing Oxford Group term "God consciousness" was relegated to second position in favor of supposed personality changes of an "educational variety." And Bill's famous "hot flash" seemed fast fading as a relic of the past. In fact, about the same time, two Roman Catholic Jesuit priests, Father Dowling and Father Ford, were reviewing and editing every line of Bill's *Twelve Steps and Twelve Traditions*—further modifying "God" as merely an option—the A.A. group being another "higher power."

The Further Revisions Through Publishing Entities

When A.A.was founded, and in the early years, there was no national office. There was no publishing entity. There was no basic text. There were no Steps. There was simply the Bible, prayer, conversion, fellowship and witness, coupled with some of the practices of the Oxford Group involving the Four Absolutes, the 5 C's, and restitution. Even these were Biblical in origin and content.

The original A.A. Step program, fashioned by Bill Wilson and published in 1939, was confined to one basic text *Alcoholics Anonymous*. But the 1940's and early 1950's saw the beginning of a plethora of explanatory books, including those mentioned above, and pamphlets published at the instance of Dr. Bob in Akron; pamphlets and newsletters published by Cleveland and other areas; and finally A.A.'s own *Grapevine* and an endless stream of later pamphlets promulgated by A.A.'s New York headquarters. In addition Bill's own remarks were published by A.A. in *As Bill Sees It* NY: Alcoholics Anonymous World Services, Inc., 1967, and *The Language of the Heart.* NY: The AA Grapevine Inc., 1988. All gave rise to new interpretations and directions—far different from those in the original program.

7.

Hindrances Today Blocking the Path of Return to Original Spiritual Roots and Power

Reflections on the possibility of getting some fresh air

I've had several interesting conversations recently with people who might qualify as independent observers and yet who are looking at the entire church outreach movements and the entire mutual help group state today. One, who was a solid, active A.A., a Christian, and an admirer of Bill Wilson, asked me when I finished a seminar on A.A. history: "What's going to happen now? Are we going to be divided and split?" Another who is head of an international movement to bring young people back into the use of prayer to solve problems asked me: "Is it possible to start 'A New A.A.'?"

In both cases, my initial answer is, "No." Religion, whether at Missions or in Churches, has had a long-standing crack at the matter of dealing with alcoholics. From my extensive research, I'm convinced that earlier religious history is filled with examples of divine healing, including alcoholism. The same thing seems to be true for the Missions and the Salvation Army if you weed out the recalcitrant vagrants who merely want a free place to eat and sleep, but don't want or believe in the inclusion of Jesus Christ in their mix. With A.A., the pressures against even the semblance of a Christian organization are immense. The United States Constitution poses a real wall, and so do recent court decisions based on it. They forbid forced attendance at what they've determined is the A.A. religion. The profit-motivated interests that fill the therapy rooms, the insurance companies, and the treatment centers would often much rather settle, at best, for a Christian "track" (which may mean "side-track") alternative as an optional program, than to include Divine cure and God's power in their format. More money, if less religion, is probably a fair statement of their position. The same for A.A. itself. Money certainly does not drive grass roots A.A., but there is an apparent desire by the hierarchy to play pit-a-pat with book revenues, convention subsidies, professionals, and treatment people rather than to reclaim Akron's 40 man experiment for approbation.

There's something dramatically wrong with a picture that sees millions still drinking and using, and a million or so being "treated" only to return repeatedly to the wine barrel or keg.. Something wrong too with religious entities that have abandoned their role of talking about God and the Bible and garnering respect for teaching truth in mutual fellowships, instead of putting testimonials in the pulpit and forming church recovery ministries far from the A.A. model, and for every kind of human plight.

In other words, I believe strongly that there will be an A.A.—whatever its form or shape—as long as there are people who worry about alcoholism, or shove their family and friends into A.A. and the like, or utilize treatment and therapy that seems scarcely capable of existing without a 12 Step increment. There will always be a core of A.A. lovers who come and serve and help voluntarily and without pay as a daily part of their lives. So there will be an A.A. Now, will it split? Well, it already has if you look at the thousands who leave it and go to church groups, secular groups, and treatment. Also to the hundreds of other organizations that have sprung up in tandem as "other" 12 Step programs because of A.A.'s single-ness-of-purpose dogma. Tell them they can't come to A.A., that there's a 12 Step N.A. program of Cocaine Anonymous program nearby; and they can and do leave.

But my concern has always been to rescue the Christian who is in A.A., allow him to be cured through his faith, and encourage him to witness to other AAs who are bumbling along in meetings, drunkalogs, dating, dancing, and apathy. Many Christians in A.A. are often disgusted with religious intolerance, but they neither leave A.A., nor support it. Their talents are simply lost.

I think there is a New Way. It's a way which may never meet with approval of some churches or of some AAs and mutual help members.

But it's a way that can draw on the best of both groups—a way that was favored in early A.A., and a way that builds on successes instead of standing on failures.

But there are hindrances to its potential, to its existence, and to its success today. Sick people don't necessarily want to fight or to debate or to choose between alternatives. Many resist any change, saying: "It works; so don't fix it." But it doesn't work. "Recovery" is missing out on God. It is missing out on prayer. It is missing out on the Bible. It is missing out on inspiring teachers and leaders. In fact, it is missing out on the best of early A.A. and the best of the many groups which served as A.A. role modes. It seems to be oblivious to history.

The Obstacles To Moderate Solutions Today

There are a number of obstacles standing in the way of early A.A.'s three-legged platform: Medicine, Religion, Experience. Medicine is still in its infancy when it comes to dealing with alcoholism and addiction. Religion—lacking both knowledge and experience—is nonetheless crowding more and more into the Experience leg. And if A.A. be called the Experience leg, it is more and more crowding both medicine and religion out of the picture. Sarcastically. Belligerently. Authoritatively. But the A.A. leg is getting wobbly. Experience didn't create the heavens and the earth. Experience didn't write the sermon on the mount. Experience alone can't interpret the Bible, fashion prayers, talk to and hear from our Creator, or define what the love of God is.

The Challenge of A.A.'s Mere 1 to 5% Success Rate Today

Despite occasional protests primarily within the A.A. fellowship, it is no secret that the original documented 75% to 93% success rate in the pioneer program has been replaced by a 1 to 5% success rate today. Though the reasons could be several, the fact is that the A.A. of today is not the A.A. of yesteryear. And this makes a review of the early history a matter of great import. Yet AAs themselves are often in super denial of their revolving numbers and tiny successes.

The Flight to Other Ideas and Programs

For a variety of reasons, the original, unique, altruistic, non-profit love and service of the A.A. pioneers and some of their successors, have been replaced with fewer and fewer examples of working with others, fewer and fewer qualified sponsors, more and more treatment programs, detached half-way houses, other support groups, mandated attendance, costly therapy, and billions of dollars in grants for research—coupled with billions spent on wars against drugs..

Christians in A.A. have flocked to other recovery organizations—some based on the Twelve Steps, and some not. Among others, these include Alcoholics Victorious, Overcomers Outreach, Inc., Overcomers, Alcoholics for Christ, Teen Challenge, Celebrate Recovery, and mores.

The Atheist-Humanist Bloc

Many unbelievers, agnostics, and atheists have rejected A.A.'s religious overtones and have turned to Rational Recovery, Moderation Management, humanist, and secular approaches.

The Speck in the Sand Status of A.A. as a Recovery Panacea

The potential impact of A.A., which boasts of only a million members in the United States, has to be contrasted with the fourteen million or more people who are non-A.A. alcoholics and the seventy-five million people in American Families impacted by alcoholism. A.A. has further limited its own impact on a preponderance of its dual-addicted members with its "singleness of purpose" doctrine which tends to exclude those with problems other than alcohol and force them to other fellowships with addiction, "substance abuse," "chemical dependency" and like problems—gambling, smoking, drugs, sexual aberrations, ADD, etc.

Moreover science, medicine, scholarship, and sociology are catching up to knowledge of the complexity of today's scene. A.A. has not held up well in scientific comparisons of its successes with those of other groups or even with those who simply quit on their own

The Revisionist Ideas and Intrusions

As A.A. has changed, the intrusions into its ideas have multiplied. The original program was about the Creator and reliance upon Him. The founders said so explicitly. Today AAs are told they may believe in whatever they wish or nothing at all. The original program included acceptance of Christ. Today the very mention of Jesus Christ in many meetings brings immediate intimidation and reproof. The original program took its basic ideas from the Bible—particularly the Book of James, 1 Corinthians 13, and the Sermon on the Mount. Today these go unmentioned. The original program incorporated the four standards of Jesus—Absolute Honesty, Absolute Purity, Absolute Unselfishness, and Absolute Love—thought to be based on the standards or yardsticks taught by Jesus Christ and spelled out in the 1800's by Dr. Robert E. Speer. Today, one would be hard-put at many a meeting to find any emphasis at all on "purity"—considering the vulgar language, overt sexual references, and frequent mention of "relationships" and "adultery." The original program actually circulated religious devotionals, books, and pamphlets. Today A.A. itself pushes only "Conference Approved" literature. The original program was self-supporting and self-governing. Today's A.A.—at the national level—is utterly dependent upon revenues from book publishing and distribution and even outside subsidies; while self-government has been retired in favor of trustees and delegates whose actions are far removed from people in the fellowship. The original program offered hospitalization, food and shelter, and family activities. Today these are relegated to insurance companies, non-profit organizations, government agencies, counseling, and groups like Al-Anon.

And the language has changed. New ideas such as "higher power" and "spirituality" and "not-god-ness" have replaced Bible verses and cut members adrift when it comes to understanding meanings. The original requirements of belief in God, conversion to Christ, Bible study, prayer meetings, Quiet Time, reading of religious literature, and medical attention are just plain missing from the fellowship.

This is not to say that you cannot today, in A.A., believe in Almighty God, claim Jesus Christ as your Lord and Saviour, read the Bible, pray, have a Quiet Time of your own, obey God' commandments, embrace the Sermon on the Mount, and attend a church and

51

denomination of your own choice. I do. Many of the people I have sponsored do. You can! But none of these activities are looked on as "part" of the A.A. program though each used to be. In fact, some people and groups who observe these practices are banned from official A.A. meeting lists. One group in Maine seeks to ban "Christian Fellowship" from language that can be spoken at an A.A. meeting.

Yet this is not the A.A. I joined, nor the A.A.I love, nor the fellowship that offered me personally so much support and non-judgmental love and service when I really needed it. The principles are not lost. They are available. They need to be recalled to mind. And they need to be considered as options in A.A., support groups, recovery groups, church groups, and treatment.

Hindrances to Historical Values--Emanating From A Present-day Focus on A.A. Shortcomings, Treatment alternatives, Singleness of Purpose, Universalism, Secularism, Rigidity, and "Spirituality"

There is no need for, or value here in, outlining the foregoing factors that seem to have led to diminishing 12 Step effectiveness. The focus on self-centeredness as a sin has replaced transgression of God's commandments as the measure of sin. The focus on treatment as a solution has replaced reliance on the Creator. The focus on drunkalogs and meeting attendance has not kept newcomers from relapses and departures. A.A.'s focus on only one type of addiction—alcoholism-- has pushed droves of "alcoholic/addicts" into other programs. The attempt to universalize A.A., as Lois Wilson urged, and to be all things to all people, has contributed to revolt against the mentioning of A.A.'s Christian roots. Angry, insulting, intimidating letters, phone calls, and remarks at meetings leave the timid seemingly baffled, suppressed, or acquiescing. The secularism, now permeating American political talk, has had its impact in A.A.—encouraging boldness by those who reject God, Jesus, the Bible, church, religion, and religious literature. Then there's what some have called the "rigidity" in the fellowship in which pull-up-the-ladder AAs urge the guardians of A.A. Traditions to "enforce" rules from above as they interpret them. And this ex cathedra mentality has diminished the respect for local group autonomy, anonymity, and the Creator as the only judge. "Spirituality"—New Age compromise talk—has become the darling of

52

those who don't want to mention God or the Bible or religion. And though the meaning of "spirituality" is totally obscure, the word has been used like a sledge hammer to drive down any religious talk. And the hammer-wielders are more often than not "historians," "scholars," professionals, and writers. They are seldom to be found in or near the trenches where AAs who have called for and received deliverance through the power of God are helping wet drunks. If "love and tolerance" is the code of the detractors, they don't show it. If "Live and Let Live" is their slogan, they've ignored it. And if "Let go and Let God" is still on the walls of the rooms they used to frequent, they just don't seem to get it.

The A.A. of today is not the A.A. of yesteryear. And the aberrations, errors, nonsense, and weaknesses of A.A. need to be learned, known, acknowledged and dealt with—but not necessarily by desertion. I'm 81 years old, 20 years sober, and as unwilling as ever to bite the hand that fed me. I know what A.A. can do. I know what it offered me. I know what it did for me. And I know what it expected of me. Best of all, I know how delightful these golden years have been when compared to the costly, desolate, damaging years of my drunkenness. I concur with the legendary prayer of the infamous Gert Behanna, which went something like this: "Dear Lord, I'm not the person you want me to be; I'm not the person I ought to be; but thank you that I'm not the person I used to be."

And I'm about to suggest that the best, new, way out of the alcoholism/addiction muddle is to offer information and choice. And the recruiter's uniform. The information is that A.A. and many organizations from which it drew its ideas have worked with high degrees of success as they relied on the Creator for help. The choice is something I'll discuss in a moment. But I believe it must be a choice that enables the teaching, learning, evaluating, and—if appropriate—applying of history. You can do it by reading. You can by listening. You can do it by applying it in your own church, your own fellowship, your own treatment program, your own group, and your own meeting. And you don't need anyone's permission. You just have to know enough about God to know He loves; enough about God to know you don't have to be a theologian to become one of His kids; enough about the Bible to recognize that it contains such a wealth of relevant truth that it was called the "Good Book"; enough about freedom in America and in A.A. to know that it's OK to think, that it's OK to reason, that it's OK to make up your own mind about God; and that the recovery pen is about the last place in the world to look for solid information about Him. Then there's recruitment. I've organized, led, and belonged to lots of organizations in my day, from Cub Scouts to high school bands, to Army squads, to Law Review researchers, to church every member fund drives. But I don't think I've ever seen an organization that offers so much to so many for so little in cost as Alcoholics Anonymous. Perhaps the greatest offer is the opportunity to help and comfort and love and support human beings at their lowest ebb—people who are emotionally, physically, mentally, spiritually, and morally sick. Sick and suffering. Sick and despairing. Sick and lonely. Sick and fearful. Sick and ashamed. Sick and suicidal. Sick and broke and hungry and often without means. There, my reader friends, is where you recruit. Jesus was described at Calvary Mission as the Carpenter who mends broken hearts. And he did a lot more than that. Still can! And you want a fulfilling, joyous, enriching experience—go and recruit a newcomer. It may be the hardest sell of your life. It may require hours and hours of time and bundles of patience. But read the Book of James and see how the reward is described.

Know how people got well in yesteryear. Read. Listen. Form a Group. Pray. Study. Believe. And remember what Ephesians 6:20 says: "Now unto Him that is able to do exceeding abundantly above all that we ask or think, according to the power that worketh in us." It's a prayer. It's a praise. It's a truth. God can pull you out of any mire or tell you where to climb. You don't need to limit God, for He tells us: "With God, nothing is impossible." You need the information that your predecessors had when they turned to God for help at the bottom of the well and found deliverance in miraculous ways. Honest! Without that history, you'll just be listening to the complaints of people who don't know or care or believe. Or think you do either. The much-decorated, wounded combat veteran who returns to help his buddies or recruit new helpers is a dynamo that can't be stopped. To get well, recruit. To stay well, recruit. To serve, train recruiters. It's about serving and glorifying our Heavenly Father because A.A. can and should offer God!

8.

The Importance of Choice

People who are suffering from alcoholism, addictions, and life-controlling problems need a choice, whether they seem to deserve it or not.

Not a mandate.

You cannot mandate abstinence. You cannot mandate resistance to temptation. You cannot mandate belief in God or His son. You cannot mandate Bible study or prayer. You cannot mandate obedience to God's commandments. You cannot mandate unselfish love and service to others. Nor can you mandate recovery by arrest, by raids, by imprisonment, by treatment, by therapy, by religion, by church, or by medicine. Nor by food, shelter, and a shower. Nor even by attacking drug lords abroad.

But you can offer a choice.

In fact, you can offer that choice through the testimony, experience, and successes others have achieved. Message-carrying is still a tool of great force. You can share about successes in any of the foregoing circumstances. And the ability to choose which message to carry and what might cause the offeree to make a good choice often depends on knowledge of the alternatives and their effectiveness. History speaks to us loudly on all these matters. How well did the Salvation Army do? How well did Christian Endeavor do? How about the YMCA? The missions? Early A.A. in Akron?

Then how well or poorly are the 12 Step programs doing? How well are the Christian programs doing? How well are the white-knuckle people doing? How well are the doctors, the researchers, the psychologists, the clergy, and others doing. History speaks loudly on these matters also. As Dr. Phil would ask: "How's that working for you!"

Christian Endeavor societies were effective. They grew in membership to 3,500,000 young people affiliated with churches around the globe; and it is reviving itself in this 125th Anniversary of its founding. The Salvation Army was effective, became known as the number one recovery program, and still seems to stand as the most effective treatment program around. Certainly the largest! Changed though it is, YMCA evangelism once reached out around the world, and the organization is large and ubiquitous today. The Oxford Group was effective for a time, even among those alcoholics who used its program; and it once sported a large following in the hundreds of thousands. The Gospel Missions, hundreds of them, are still holding out their compassion and message. And early A.A.'s pioneer program itself achieved unusual effectiveness—beginning with a tiny pilot group known as the "First Forty" who were "medically incurable" and deemed 100% hopeless without Divine Help.

A.A.'s own "Conference Approved" literature affirms early A.A. effectiveness. The claims are set forth in the forewords to the basic texts. But today's publications just don't itemize the history or the details or the ingredients in such a way that AAs as a whole are attracted. That's strange when you remember that we are still talking about George Washington, Ben Franklin, Abe Lincoln, Alexander Graham Bell, Marconi, Eli Whitney, George Washington Carver, FDR, Martin Luther King, Albert Einstein, and Dwight Eisenhower. They made their mark. We know what they did. And we're not too timid to mention them. In fact, we frequently teach about them.

Actually, A.A.'s conference approved literature does tell us this about Dr. Bob:

(1) "The birth of our Society dates from his first day of permanent sobriety, June 10, 1935. To 1950, the year of his death, he carried the A.A. message to more than 5,000 alcoholic men and women, and to all these he gave his medical services without thought of charge." (*Alcoholics Anonymous*, 4th ed., p. 171). Not bad for a dude who wallowed in his cups until late in life!

56

(2) "It had been decided that Bob would attend mostly to the questions of hospitalization and the development of our Twelfth Step work. Between 1940 and 1950, in the company of that marvelous nun, Sister Ignatia, Bob had **treated 5,000 drunks** at St. Thomas Hospital in Akron. His spiritual example was a powerful influence, and he never charged a cent for his medical care. So Dr. Bob **became the prince of all twelfth-steppers.** Perhaps nobody will ever do such a job again." (*The Co-Founders of Alcoholics Anonymous: Biographical Sketches: Their Last Major Talks.* NY: Alcoholics Anonymous World Services, Inc., 1972, 1975, p. 34. bold face added). Not bad for a physician who might well have lost his license had he continued drinking to excess!

(3) Bob's personal story concluded: "If you think you are an atheist, an agnostic, a skeptic, or have any other form of intellectual pride which keeps you from accepting what is in this book, I feel sorry for you. . . we know we have an answer for you. It never fails, if you go about it with one-half the zeal you have been in the habit of showing when you were getting another drink. **Your Heavenly Father will never let you down!**" (*Alcoholics Anonymous*, 4th ed., p. 181. bold face added). Pretty convincing coming from an alcoholic who had the credentials to make such a claim—based on his own life, and the lives of thousands he touched.

A.A.'s Conference Approved literature reports as to the early program the following documented success rates among medically incurable alcoholics who really tried:

(1) "Of alcoholics who came to A.A. and really tried, 50% got sober at once and remained that way; 25% sobered up after some relapses. . . ." (*Alcoholics Anonymous*, 4th ed., p. xx)—And the Akron success rate **was 75%!** Not bad for a new organization with only 40 members!

(2) "Records in Cleveland show that 93 percent of those who came to us never had a drink again." (*DR. BOB and the Good Oldtimers*, p. 261). The Cleveland Groups grew from one to thirty in a year. And the Cleveland success rate **was**

93%. Not bad for a spin-off gang whose beginnings came out of a revolt!

Was there "A Way Out" in those early days for those who really tried? Well who wouldn't sign up for a way out that was paved primarily by a doctor who had treated over 5,000 drunks, achieved a 75% success rate, and sponsored a man (Clarence Snyder) whose groups achieved a 93% success rate and grew to a total of 30 groups in a year! Not bad for pupils who picked up the best of that day—the Bible, the Four Absolutes, the Big Book, and the Twelve Steps—and made them sing. Then humbly gave God the credit.

Moreover, these people—all of them— were cured. And the best proof of that can be found in another quote from A.A. "Conference Approved" literature where Bill Wilson explicitly spelled out the golden text of A.A. when Bill said to Henrietta Dotson, wife of A.A. Number Three:

> "Henrietta, the Lord has been so wonderful to me, curing me of this terrible disease, that I just want to keep talking about it and telling people." (*Alcoholics Anonymous*, 4th ed., p. 191). Not bad for a former atheist stock broker and an almost dead lawyer.

Wouldn't you prefer and choose a program where the first three members were "cured," where they said so explicitly, where they had been pronounced "medically incurable," and where they boldly declared that the Lord had cured them?

You bet there's a choice. Today! Just learn the history. Compare the results today. And ask what you have to do to make the choice and receive the results.

9.

The Choice of A New Way Out

Learn the History

Find out which the early recovery feeder sources were, whom they helped, and what they did. Don't settle for gossip or rumor. Get the facts! What approaches to overcoming human need and spiritual suffering were taken by the Salvation Army, Christian Endeavor, the YMCA, the Gospel Missions, the Oxford Group, and the early A.A. Pioneers. Find the common elements in their respective efforts. Today we have the un-edited, un-compromised history. Learn it.

Learn about the immense number of healings and cures from earliest Biblical times to the present. Find out who accomplished them, whom they helped, and what they did. Learn how much God, His son, the Apostles, and believers were able to help the afflicted through offering salvation, the Bible, prayer, and compassion. Clergy assisted. They were the teachers of early A.A. What happened to them? Learn that the dead were raised; lepers were cleansed; the blind were given sight; the deaf given hearing; the dumb given speech; and the lame given wholeness. Learn this history. The healings are still going on today. They did in A.A., and they can today.

Recognize and be able to label the spurious manufactured nonsense in present-day recovery fellowships—half-baked prayers, self-made religion, absurd names for God, illusory "spirituality," and meaningless "cosmic" chatter. Learn it. Spot it. Spit it back with history.

Recognize and reject the erroneous statements about A.A. history and A.A. beliefs that are made by atheists and clerics alike. If they criticize

A.A., make sure they've correctly stated the facts, rather than manufactured them to suit their own resentments, prejudices, and doctrines. Make sure they are talking about *your A.A., your meetings, your group, your program, and your beliefs.* You can criticize and sympathize in today's A.A. But you sure can't generalize. We have a lot of different pigeons with a lot of different feathers flying in a lot of different directions to a lot of different places. Learn where your birds of a feather are flying. And flock!

Don't Leave It. Use It

If some poor jerk tells you that your higher power can be a light bulb, just don't turn on that light. Don't leave the room. Don't leave A.A. Just go to where the light is. God is light, and in Him is no darkness at all. (1 John 1:5). Just choose to walk in the light, as God is light, rather than walk in darkness. As quickly as you can, learn what God has to say on any matter. Jerry Dunn laid that out pretty plainly—get them to the Gospel as quickly as you can. But stay with the ship. There are plenty of believers on it and in it; there are plenty of people who help and serve whether they believe or not; and there are hordes coming in who need all the light, all the believing, and all the help you can provide. A.A. is a place where you can become fishers of men—people desperately seeking and hoping for help. And by the way, how many people would have signed up with Jesus or Paul at first blush. These men were recruiters!

If some poor jerk tells you that A.A. traditions forbid your believing in, talking about, or telling others about God, Jesus Christ, the Bible, and the gift of the Holy Spirit, just don't buy it. Learn your history. Stand on what AAs have done all seventy-five years of their existence. In the beginning, they were a Christian Fellowship; they believed that God is; they studied the Bible; they prayed; they sought God's guidance; they urged that God's will be done; and they threw in the practical one—faith without works is dead. No faith, no works. So there must have been faith. Bring your precious newcomer to faith in God just as quickly as you can; and show him the pages in the Big Book that support you.

If some poor jerk tells you that the Bible or a hymnal or a prayer or a religious tract is not "Conference Approved" literature, agree with him. Then ask him how it is that every early A.A. meeting was conducted by a leader with an open Bible in his lap. And that the Book of James, the Sermon on the Mount, and 1 Corinthians 13 were considered absolutely essential to the program. Ask him where those things are declared to be "conference dis-approved." The silence will be deafening.

How To Use It

The "New Way Out" is loaded with signposts. Some tell you not to drink and to go to meetings. Nothing bad about that. Some tell you to study the Big Book and take the Twelve Steps. Nothing bad about that. Some tell you to get a sponsor and keep in close touch. Nothing wrong with that. Some tell you to get a commitment setting up chairs or making coffee. Nothing wrong with that. Some tell you to get a mop and clean up after the meeting. Nothing wrong with that. Some tell you to stay away from slippery people and slippery places. Nothing wrong with that. Some tell you to stick with the winners. Nothing wrong with that. Some tell you alcoholics can have fun. Nothing wrong with that. Why dump all that when it's going on almost 24 hours a day in almost every city and rural area in America. The road sign that points to A.A. or some similar Twelve Step Fellowship is pointing in the right direction if you want to choose that path.

The "New Way Out" is loaded with other signposts. Some tell you to believe in God. Nothing wrong with that. Some tell you to get born again of God's spirit. Nothing wrong with that. Some tell you to study God's Word. Nothing wrong with that—particularly since A.A. itself got all its basic ideas from the Bible. Some tell you to pray. Nothing wrong with that. Some tell you to seek God's guidance. Nothing wrong with that. Some tell you to read religious literature. Nothing wrong with that. Some tell you to talk with *your* minister, rabbi, or priest. Nothing wrong with that. Some tell you to go regularly to a church of *your* choice. Nothing wrong with that. Some tell you to fellowship with like-minded believers. Nothing wrong with that. Some tell you to witness to unbelievers and non-believers. Nothing wrong with that—since that how it all began in many places. The road sign that points to church, or a Bible fellowship, or a religious retreat, or to Bible study is pointing in the right direction if you want to choose that path.

Now the question is: Can you choose to walk on both paths? And the answer certainly is "yes." You can participate in A.A. and in church all the time any time. Dr. Bob did. You can participate in A.A. and read the Bible every day. Dr. Bob did. You can pray for yourself and for others any time. Dr. Bob did. You can read the Big Book and take the Twelve Steps as soon as possible. Clarence Snyder did. He took his people through the Big Book and the Twelve Steps in two days, sometimes in an afternoon. You can speak at A.A. meetings, participate in conferences, write articles, and sponsor AAs all the time. Clarence Snyder did. He also went to church, read the Bible regularly, and prayed for and with people. The road sign that points to your taking both paths is pointing to a well-worn route if you want to make that choice. The beauty of it all is that you can have one foot in each path or both feet in each path, but not both feet in both paths. Choose when and where to walk. It's your choice.

But by now you should see this is A New Way Out. It used to be the only way out. But today people tend to polarize. It's A.A. or else. It's church or else. Why? If each knew more history and knew more about the other and understood how much each can help the other, that's a way you could willingly choose and walk. I have chosen it. And I've learned to expect and stand against the fiery darts of an adversary who wants to defeat A.A. and the church. And when I say church, I am really talking about God and His son Jesus Christ and the body of Christ. And that battle was won on the Cross centuries back.

We Can Provide Specific Information

History has been my dedication for 17 years. Membership in, and working with, drunks has been my continuing outreach. Growth in fellowship with our Heavenly Father, His son, and believers has been a regular objective, coupled with a continuing quest for the truth found in God's Word and from such revelation as He chooses to provide to His kids. I love it all. It's what life really has to offer today—even out here on the shores and sands of beautiful Maui, Hawaii.

With completion of this title, we will have published 29 titles covering every aspect of early A.A.'s history and spiritual roots. These are available as a reference set at a discount. We have written 160 articles as part of ongoing insight and research, and dictated over 60 audio talks to supplement the material. We keep up to date on religious matters, recovery matters, and 12 Step matters. And we post our findings on our four websites, the main one having over one million three hundred thousand visits. And most of our literature and other materials are distributed free so that the afflicted can really learn, whatever their financial straits. Our charitable work is enabled by twenty or so benefactors who wish to contribute financially to what we do. And there are the volunteers—hundreds of them—all over the world who continually help.

We urge you to let us provide you with a chapter of history as an element of your program, whether it is your own program, a program you are sponsoring, a program of your church, a therapy or treatment or rehab program, an agency or information outreach, or one of the many arms that belong to the body of Christ and are ever trying to help.

Incorporate an Historical Segment in Your Thinking and Program

Get the Ingredients of the Creator's Power and Cures Back Into Focus

And here were the original ingredients of the cures the early Akron A.A. Christian Fellowship offered and embraced:

(1) The choice of abstinence,

(2) The choice of avoiding temptation,

(3) The choice of entrusting one's life to the care, direction, and strength of the Creator,

(4) The choice of establishing a relationship with Him through Christ,

(5) The choice of obeying His commandments and eliminating sinful conduct,

63

(6) The choice of growing in knowledge and fellowship with Him, His son, and His children through Bible study, prayer, religious fellowship, worship, and witness.

(7) The choice of passing along to others with love and service the message that will enable those others to help and be helped in like manner.

Utilize the history and ingredients whatever be your need and wherever you belong:

You may, if you choose, apply the principles of the early programs wherever you are. Buy, if you will, our belief that Old-time religion, Old-time moral precepts, and Old-School A.A. work successfully in any one's life when such ideas are grounded on the truth in God's Word. You can apply them in your church, in your Bible fellowship, in your recovery group, in your treatment program, in Alcoholics Anonymous, in 12 Step programs, in your youth groups, in your outreach to prisoners, in jail or prison, in mental health facilities, among the homeless, the abandoned, and their families and children. And, yes, in your workplace, jobsite, and business. And it's time to learn the facts, keep your powder dry, and start walking, using A New Way Out.

Conclusion

There is an opportunity today for those who want to pick up the mantle. It requires choices, enthusiastic participation, adequate instruction, unselfish personal outreach, a message of truth, a faith in God, and an underlying love of God in action. It is available to and for youngsters. It is available through and for churches and non-profits. It is available through and for treatment. It is available in and for anonymous and 12 Step groups. It is available in and through recovery groups and programs. It can be made available in prisons and jails, in mental health facilities, homeless and support groups, and in educational courses. With today's effective communication alternatives, it can be made available on TV, radio, video, audio, CD, DVD, websites, blog sites, and even cell phones. It can be made available in meetings, groups, conferences, seminars, panels, cruises, retreats, camps, and a host of other areas. Its time has come,

And I know we have the resources that can enable you to do your share right now. I also want you to know that we will always welcome your help and financial support. Books and computers and cameras don't grow on trees! Neither do tickets or meals. And may God bless you and show you A New Way Out if you choose to learn and activate it.

End
Gloria Dei

Bibliography

Alcoholics Anonymous. New Jersey: Works Publishing Company, 1939 [the "First Edition"]

Alcoholics Anonymous, 2d ed. NY: Alcoholics Anonymous World Services, Inc., 1956

Alcoholics Anonymous, 3rd ed. NY: Alcoholics Anonymus World Services, Inc., 1975

Alcoholics Anonymous, 4th ed. NY: Alcoholics Anonymous World Services, Inc., 2002.

Alcoholics Anonymous Comes of Age. NY: Alcoholics Anonymous World Services, Inc., 1957.

A Guide to the Twelve Steps of Alcoholics Anonymous. Akron: AA of Akron, n.d.

A Manual for Alcoholics Anonymous, rev. ed. AA of Akron, 1989

AA Grapevine, The: *"RHS"* - issue dedicated to the memory of the Co-Founder of Alcoholics Anonymous, DR. BOB. NY: The AA Grapevine, Inc., 1951.

Allen, A. A. *How To Have Power Over The Devil.* AZ: A. A. Allen Revivals, Inc., 1954.

Allen, James. *As a Man Thinketh.* NY: Peter Pauper Press, Inc., n.d.

Anderson, Bernard W. *Understanding The Old Testament.* NJ: Prentice Hall, 1957.

A Newcomer Asks. . . York, England: A.A. Sterling Area Services, n.d.

B., Dick. *Anne Smith's Journal, 1933-1939*, 3rd ed. Kihei, HI: Paradise Research Publications, Inc., 1998

_____. *By the Power of God: A Guide to Early A.A. Groups & Similar Groups Today.* Kihei, HI: Paradise Research Publications, Inc., 2000.

_____. *Cured!: Proven Help for Alcoholics and Addicts.* Kihei, HI: Paradise Research Publications, Inc., 2003.

_____. *Dr. Bob and His Library*, 3rd ed., Kihei, HI: Paradise Research Publications, Inc., 1998

_____. *God and Alcoholism: Our Growing Opportunity in the 21st Century*. Kihei, HI: Paradise Research Publications, Inc., 2002.

_____. *Good Morning!: Quiet Time, Morning Watch, Meditation, and Early A.A.*, 2d ed. Kihei, HI: Paradise Research Publications, Inc., 1998.

_____. *Henrietta Seiberling: Ohio's Lady with a Cause.* Kihei, HI: Paradise Research Publications, Inc., 2004.

_____. *Making Known the Biblical History and Roots of Alcoholics Anonymous.* Kihei, HI: Paradise Research Publications, Inc., 2006.

_____. *New Light on Alcoholism: God, Sam Shoemaker, and A.A.*, 2d ed. Kihei, HI: Paradise Research Publications, Inc., 1999.

_____. *The Akron Genesis of Alcoholics Anonymous*, 2d ed. Kihei, HI: Paradise Research Publications, Inc., 1998.

_____. *The Books Early AAs Read for Spiritual Growth*, 7th ed. Kihei, HI: Paradise Research Publications, Inc., 1998.

_____. *The Conversion of Bill W.: More on the Creator's Role in Early A.A.* HI: Paradise Research Publications, Inc., 2006.

_____. *The First Nationwide A.A. History Conference*. HI Paradise Research Publications, Inc., 2005

_____. *The Golden Text of A.A.: God, the Pioneers, and Real Spirituality*. Kihei, HI: Paradise Research Publications, Inc., 1999.

_____. *The Good Book and The Big Book: A.A.'s Roots in the Bible*, 2d ed. Kihei, HI: Paradise Research Publications, Inc., 1997.

_____. *The Good Book-Big Book Guidebook*. HI: Paradise Research Publications, Inc., 2006.

_____. *The James Club and The Original A.A. Program's Absolute Essentials* HI: Paradise Research Publications, Inc., 2006.

_____. *The Oxford Group and Alcoholics Anonymous*, 2d ed. Kihei, HI: Paradise Research Publications, Inc., 1998.

_____. *That Amazing Grace* (Clarence & Grace S.). Kihei, HI: Paradise Research Publications, Inc., 1996.

_____. *Turning Point: A History of Early A.A.'s Spiritual Roots and Successes*. Kihei, HI: Paradise Research Publications, Inc., 1997.

_____. *Twelve Steps for You.*. HI: Paradise Research Publications, Inc., 2005)

_____. *Utilizing Early A.A.'s Spiritual Roots for Recovery Today*, Rev. ed. Kihei, HI: Paradise Research Publications, Inc., 1999.

_____. *When Early AAs Were Cured and Why*. HI: Paradise Research Publications, Inc., 2006.

_____. *Why Early A.A. Succeeded: The Good Book in Alcoholics Anonymous Yesterday and Today (A Bible Study Primer)*. Kihei, HI: Paradise Research Publications, Inc., 2001.

B., Mel. *New Wine: The Spiritual Roots of the Twelve Step Miracle*. Hazelden, 1991.

_____. *My Search for Bill W*. MN: Hazelden, 2000.

Begbie, Harold. *Life Changers*. NY: G. P. Putnam's Sons, 1927.

_____. *The Gospel Truth: Life of William Booth, Founder and First General of the Salvation Army*, 2 vol.

_____. *Twice Born Men*. NY: Fleming H. Revell, 1909.

Best of the Grapevine, Volume II. NY: The AA Grapevine, Inc., 1986.

Bobgan, Martin and Deidre. 12 Steps to Destruction: Codependency Recovery Heresies. Santa Barbara, CA: EastGate Publishers, 1991.

Bosworth, F. F. *Christ The Healer*. MI: Fleming H. Revell, 1996.

Brown, Kenneth O. *Holy Ground, Too: The Camp Meeting Family Tree*. PA: Holiness Archives, 1997.

Brown, William. *Personality and Religion*. London: University of London Press, Ltd., 1946.

Bruns, Roger A. *Preacher Billy Sunday and Big-Time American Evangelism*. Urbana: University of Illinois Press, 1992.

Burns, Dr. Cathy. *Alcoholics Anonymous Unmasked: Deception and Deliverance*. Mt. Carmel, PA: Sharing, 1991.

Bushnell, Horace. *The New Life*. London: Strahan & Co., 1868.

C., Stewart. *A Reference Guide to the Big Book of Alcoholics Anonymous*. Seattle: Recovery Press, 1986.

Cabot, Richard C. and Russell L. Dicks. *The Art of Ministering to the Sick*. NY: The Macmillan Company, 1946.

Chambers, Oswald. *My Utmost for His Highest*. Oswald Chambers Publishing Assn., 1963.

_____. *Studies in the Sermon on the Mount*. MI: Discovery House, 1960.

Clapp, Charles, Jr. *The Big Bender*. NY: Harper & Row, 1938.

Clark, Francis E. *Christian Endeavor in All Lands.* N.p.: The United Society of Christian Endeavor, 1906.

_____. *Memoirs of Many Men in Many Lands: An Autobiography.* Boston: United Society of Christian Endeavor, 1922.

Clark, Glenn. *How to Find Health Through Prayer.* NY: Harper & Row, 1940.

Cleveland Central Bulletin. Volumes I - III Cleveland Central Committee, Oct/42 - Dec/45.

Clinebell, Howard. *Understanding and Counseling Persons with Alcohol, Drug, and Behavioral Addictions.* Rev. and enl. ed. Nashville: Abingdon Press, 1998.

Comparative Study Bible. Rev ed. MI: Zondervan Publishing House, 1999.

Complete Jewish Bible. Clarksville, MD: Jewish New Testament Publications, Inc., 1998.

Daily, Starr. *Recovery.* Minnesota: Macalester Park Publishing, 1948.

_____. *Release.* NY : Harper & Brothers, 1942

Darrah, Mary C. *Sister Ignatia: Angel of Alcoholics Anonymous.* Chicago: Loyola University Press, 1992.

Dawson, George Gordon. *Healing: Pagan and Christian.* London: Society For Promoting Christian Knowledge, 1935.

Day, Sherwood Sunderland. *The Principles of the Group.* Oxford: University Press, n.d.

Dearmer, Percy. *Body and Soul: An Enquiry into the Effects of Religion Upon Health, With a Description of Christian Works of Healing From the New Testament to the Present Day.* London: Sir Isaac Pitman & Sons, Ltd., 1909.

DR. BOB and the Good Oldtimers. NY: Alcoholics Anonymous World Services, Inc., 1980.

Drummond, Henry. *The Greatest Thing in the World.* Fleming H. Revell, 1968.

_____. *The Ideal Life.* NY: Dodd, Mead and Company, 1898.

Dunn, Jerry. *God is for the Alcoholic.* Chicago: Moody Press, 1965.

E., Bob. *Handwritten Note to Lois Wilson on pamphlet entitled "Four Absolutes."* (Copy made available to author by Founders Day Archivist, Akron, Ohio, in June, 1991)

_____. Letter from Bob E. to Nell Wing. NY: Stepping Stones Archives, Bedford Hills, NY.

Eddy, Mary Baker. *Science and Health with Key to the Scriptures.* Boston: Published by the Trustees under the Will of Mary Baker Eddy, 1916.

Ellis, William T. *Billy Sunday: The Man and His Message.* Chicago: Moody Press, 1959.

Fillmore, Charles. *Christian Healing.* Kansas City: Unity School of Christianity, 1936.

Fillmore, Charles and Cora. *Teach Us to Pray.* MO: Unity School of Christianity, 1945.

Forde, Eleanor Napier. *Guidance: What It Is and How to Get It.* Paper presented by Eleanor Napier Forde at Minnewaska, New York, September, 1927.

_____. *The Guidance of God.* London: The Oxford Group, 1927.

Fosdick, Harry Emerson. *The Man from Nazareth: As His Contemporaries Saw Him.* NY: Harper & Brothers, 1949.

_____. *The Meaning of Prayer.* NY: Association Press, 1915.

Fox, Emmet. *Find and Use Your Inner Power.* NY: Harper & Brothers, 1937.

_____. *Getting Results by Prayer* (pamphlet, 1933).

_____. *Power through Constructive Thinking.* NY: Harper & Brothers, 1932.

_____. *The Sermon on the Mount.* New York: Harper & Row, 1934.

67

Frame, Hugh F. *Wonderful, Counsellor: A Study in the Life of Jesus.* London: Hodder And Stoughton Limited, 1935.

Frost, Evelyn. *Christian Healing: A Consideration of the Place of Spiritual Healing in the Church of To-day in the Light of the Doctrine and Practice of the Ante-Nicene Church.* London: A.R. Mobray & Co. Limited, 1940.

Gilkey, Charles Whitney. *Jesus and Our Generation.* Chicago: The University of Chicago Press, 1925.

Glover, T. R. *The Jesus of History.* New York: Association Press, 1930.

Grant, W. V. *Just Before The Healing Service.* TX: Faith Clinic, n.d.

_____. *Live all Your Life.* TX: Faith Clinic, n.d.

_____. *Power from on High.* TX: Faith Clinic, n.d.

_____. *The Grace of God in My Life.* TX: Faith Clinic, 1952.

_____. *When Prayer Fails.* TX: Grant's Faith Clinic, n.d.

Gray, Steve. *Hope Heals.* MO: World Revival Press, 2003.

Grensted, Rev. L. W. *Psychology and God: A Study of The Implications of Recent Psychology For Religious Belief and Practice.* London: Longmans, Green and Co., 1931.

_____. *The Person Of Christ.* London: Nisbet & Co., Ltd., 1933.

Guldseth, Mark. *Streams.* Alaska: Fritz Creek Studios, 1945.

Harrell, Jr., David Edwin. *Oral Roberts: An American Life* San Francisco: Harper & Row Publishers, 1985.

Hayes, Norvell. *The Healing Handbook.* Tulsa, OK: Harrison House, 1982.

Heard, Gerald. *A Preface to Prayer.* NY: Harper & Brothers, 1934.

Heiler, Friedrich. *Prayer: A Study in the History and Psychology of Religion.* Oxford: Oneworld Publications, 1932.

Herman, E. *Creative Prayer.* London: James Clarke & Co., Ltd., 1921.

Hicks, Roger. *How to Read the Bible.* London: Moral Re-Armament, 1940.

Hickson, James Moore. *Heal The Sick.* London: Methuen & Co., 1924.

Holm, Nora Smith. *The Runner's Bible.* NY: Houghton Mifflin Company, 1913.

Inman, Philip. *Christ in the Modern Hospital.* London: Hodder & Stoughton Ltd., 1937.

James, William. *The Varieties of Religious Experience.* NY: First Vintage Press/The Library of America Edition, 1990.

New Jerusalem Bible

Jones, E. Stanley. *Christ And Human Suffering.* New York: The Abingdon Press, 1930.

_____. *The Christ of the Mount.* NY: Abingdon Press, 1930.

Jung, Carl Gustav. *Modern Man In Search of a Soul.* NY: Harcourt, Brace & World, Inc., 1933.

_____. *Psychology & Religion.* New Haven: Yale University Press, 1938.

_____. *The Psychogenesis of Mental Disease.* NY: Bolingen Foundation, 1960.

K., Mitchell. *How it Worked: The Story of Clarence H. Snyder and The Early Days of Alcoholics Anonymous in Cleveland, Ohio*: NY: AA Big Book Study Group, 1997.

K., Richard. *Early A.A. - Separating Fact From Fiction: How Revisionists Have Led Our History Astray.* Haverhill, MA: Golden Text Publishing Co., 2003.

_____. *New Freedom: Reclaiming Alcoholics Anonymous. MA*: Golden Text Publishing Co., 2005

Kagawa, Toyohiko. *Love: The Law of Life.* Philadelphia: The John C. Winston Company, 1929.

Kelsey, Morton T. *Psychology, Medicine & Christian Healing.* Rev. ed. San Francisco: Harper & Row, Publishers, 1966.

Kenyon, E. W. *Jesus the Healer*. Kenyon's Gospel Publishing Society, Inc., 2000.
_____. *The True Story*. FL: Creation House, 1997.
_____. *The Wonderful Name of Jesus*. Kenyon's Gospel Publishing Society, 1998.
    King James Version, Authorized
King, J. D. *"Written Not With Ink But With the Spirit."* MO: World Revival Press, 2003
Kitchen, V. C. *I Was a Pagan*. NY: Harper & Brothers, 1934.
Kurtz, Ernest. *Not-God: A History of Alcoholics Anonymous*, Exp ed. Hazelden, 1991.
Lake, Dr. John G. Lake. *The Astounding Diary of Dr. John G. Lake*. TX: Christ for the Nations, 1987.
Laubach, Frank. *Prayer (Mightiest Force in the World)*. NY: Fleming H. Revell, 1946.
Laymon, Charles M. *A Primer of Prayer*. Nashville: Tidings, 1949.
Lewis, C. S. *Miracles: How God Intervenes in Nature and Human Affairs*. NY: Collier Books, 1960.
Liardon, Roberts. *God's Generals*. Tulsa, OK: Albury Publishing, 1996.
_____. *John G. Lake: The Complete Collection Of His Life's Teachings*. Tulsa, OK: Alsbury Publishing, 1999.
Lindsay, Gordon. *John Alexander Dowie: Champion Of The Faith*. TX: Christ for the Nations, Inc., 1987.
_____. *John G. Lake: Apostle To Africa*. TX: Christ for the Nations, 2000.
_____. *The John G. Lake Sermons*. TX: Christ for the Nations, 2002
_____. *The New John G. Lake Sermons*. TX: Christ for the Nations, 1994.
_____. *William Branham: A Man Sent From God*. IN: William Branham Evangelistic Association, n.d.
Lovett, C. S. *Jesus Wants You Well!* Baldwin Park, CA: Personal Christianity, 1973.
Lupton, Dilworth. *Religion Says You Can*. Boston: The Beacon Press, 1938.
Macmillan, Ebenezer. *Seeking and Finding*. NY: Harper & Brothers, 1933.
Maillard, John. *Healing in the Name of Jesus*. London: Hodder & Stoughton, 1936.
Markey, Morris. *Alcoholics and God*. Liberty Magazine, 1939.
McCarthy, Katherine. *The Emmanuel Movement and Richard Peabody* (Journal of Studies on Alcohol, Vol. 45, No. 1, 1984).
McIntosh, Ron. *The Quest for Revival: Experiencing Great Revivals of the Past, Empowering You for God's Move Today*. Tulsa, OK: Harrison House, 1997.
Micklem, E. R. *Miracles & The New Psychology: A Study in the Healing Miracles of the New Testament*. London: Oxford University Press, 1922.
Mitchel, Dale. *Silkworth: The Little Doctor Who Loved Drunks*. MN: Hazelden. 2002.
Moody, Dwight L. *Secret Power: Or, The Secret of Success in Christian Life and Work*. Chicago: F. H. Revell, 1881.
Mosely, Rufus. *Perfect Everything*. MN: Macalester Park Publishing, 1949.
Murch, James DeForest. *Successful C.E. Prayer-Meetings*. OH: Standard Publishing Co., 1930.
New Bible Dictionary, Second Edition. England: Inter-Varsity Press, 1982.
Newton, James Draper. *Uncommon Friends*. NY: Harcourt Brace, 1987.
Osborn, T.L. *Believers in Action*. Tulsa, OK: T. L. Osborn, 2000.
_____. *Healing the Sick*. Tulsa, OK: Harrison House, 1992.
_____. *Join This Chariot*. Tulsa, OK: Osborn Foundation, n.d.
_____. *Miracles: Proof of God's Power*. Tulsa, OK: Harrison House, 1981.
_____. Osborn, Daisy. *When Jesus Visited Our House*. Tulsa, OK: Faith Digest, 1960.

P. Wally. *But for the Grace of God*. WV: The Bishop of Books, 1995.

Parker, William R. and Elaine St. Johns. *Prayer Can Change Your Life*. New ed. NY: Prentice Hall, 1957.

Pass It On. NY: *Alcoholics Anonymous World Services*, 1984.

Paton, Wally. *How to Listen to God: A Guide to Successful Living Through the Practice of Two-way Prayer*. Tucson, AZ: Faith With Works Publishing Company, 2000.

Peabody, Richard R. *The Common Sense of Drinking*. Atlantic Monthly Press Book, 1939.

Peale, Norman Vincent. *The Positive Power of Jesus Christ*. NY: Foundation for Christian Living, 1980

_____. *The Power of Positive Thinking*. NY: Peale Center for Christian Living, 1978.

Peele, Stanton. *Diseasing of America*. Lexington, MA: Lexington Books, 1989.

_____. And Bufe, Charles. *Resisting 12-Step Coercion: How To Fight Forced Participation in AA, NA, or 12-Step Treatment*. Tucson, AZ: See Sharp Press, 1998.

Phillips, Rachel M. *Billy Sunday: Evangelist on the Sawdust Trail*. Barbour Books, 2001.

Pittman, Bill. *AA The Way It Began*. Seattle: Glen Abbey Books, 1988.

Pittman, Bill and B., Dick. *Courage to Change: The Christian Roots of the Twelve-Step Movement*. MN: Hazelden.

Poe, Stephen E. and Frances E. *A Concordance to Alcoholics Anonymous*. NV: Purple Salamander Press, 1990.

Pridie, J. R. *The Church's Ministry of Healing*. London: Society For Promoting Christian Knowledge, 1926.

Puller, F. W. *The Anointing of the Sick in Scripture and Tradition, with some Considerations on the Numbering of the Sacraments*. London: Society For Promoting Christian Knowledge, 1904.

Rawson, F. L. *The Nature of True Prayer*. England: The Society for Spreading The Knowledge of True Prayer, 1918.

Redwood, Hugh. *God in the Shadows*. London: Hodder & Stoughton, 1934.

Richardson, Alan. *The Miracle-Stories of the Gospels*. London: SCM Press Ltd, 1941.

Riss, Richard M. *A Survey of 20th-Century Revival Movements in North America*. MA: Hendrickson Publishers, 1988.

Roberts, Oral. *Expect A Miracle: My Life and Ministry*. Nashville: Thomas Nelson Publishers, 1995.

_____. *If You Need Healing Do These Things*. Tulsa, OK: Healing Waters, Inc., 1952.

_____. *Oral Roberts' Life Story*. Tulsa, OK: Oral Roberts, 1952.

Rotherham's Emphasized Bible. MI: Kegel Publications, 1994.

S., Clarence. *Going through the Steps*, 2d ed. Altamonte Springs, FL: Stephen Foreman, 1985.

_____. *My Higher Power–The Lightbulb*. 2d ed., Altamonte Springs, FL: Stephen Foreman, 1985

Schaer, Hans. *Religion and The Cure of Souls in Jung's Psychology*. NY: Bolingen Foundation, 1950.

Schaff, Philip. *History of the Christian Church, Volume I*, 3rd Revision (Grand Rapids., MI: Wm B. Eerdman's Publishing Company, 1890.

Schambach, R. W. *Demon Possession Today and How to Be Free*. TX: Schambach Revivals, Inc., 1992.

_____. *God's Guarantee to Heal You.* Tx: Schambach Revivals, 1991.

_____. *The Price of God's Miracle-Working Power.* TX: Schambach Ministries, Inc., 1991.

Second Reader for Alcoholics Anonymous. Akron: AA of Akron, n.d.

Shafto, G. R.H. *The Wonders of the Kingdom: A Study of the Miracles of Jesus.* NY: George H. Doran Company, 1924.

Shoemaker, Helen Smith. *I Stand By The Door: The Life of Sam Shoemaker.* NY: Harper & Row Publishers, 1967.

Shoemaker, Samuel M., Jr. *Children of the Second Birth.* NY: Fleming H. Revell, 1927.

_____. *Confident Faith.* NY: Fleming H. Revell, 1932.

_____. *Extraordinary Living for Ordinary Men.* MI: Zondervan Publishing House, 1965.

_____. *How To Become A Christian.* NY: Harper & Row, Publishers, 1953.

_____. "How to Find God." *The Calvary Evangel*, July, 1957.

_____. *National Awakening.* NY: Harper & Brothers, 1936.

_____. *Realizing Religion.* NY: Association Press, 1923.

_____. *One Boy's Influence.* NY: Association Press,

_____. *Religion That Works.* NY: Fleming H. Revell, 1928.

_____. *Sam Shoemaker at his best.* NY: Faith At Work, Inc., 1964.

_____. *The Church Can Save the World.* NY: Harper & Brothers, 1938

_____. *The Experiment of Faith.* NY: Harper & Brothers, 1957.

_____. *The Gospel According to You.* NY: Fleming H. Revell, 1934.

_____. *Twice-Born Ministers.* NY: Fleming H. Revell, 1929.

Smith, Bob and Sue Smith Windows. *Children of the Healer.* IL: Parkside Publishing, 1992.

Speer, Robert E. *Studies of the Man Christ Jesus.* NY: Fleming H. Revell, 1896.

_____. *The Principles of Jesus.* NY: Fleming H. Revell Company, 1902.

Spiritual Milestones in Alcoholics Anonymous. Akron: AA of Akron, n.d.

Stadsklev, Julius. *William Branham: A Prophet Visits South Africa.* MN: Julius Stadsklev, 1952.

Stafford, Tim. "The Hidden Gospel of the 12 Steps." *Christianity Today*, July 22, 1991.

Stalker, James. *The Life of Jesus Christ.* NY: Fleming H. Revell, 1891.

Streeter, B. H. *The God Who Speaks.* London: Macmillan & Co., Ltd., 1936.

Streeter, B. H. (Editor). *The Spirit: God and His Relation to Man Considered From The Standpoint of Philosophy, Psychology And Art.* London: Macmillan And Co., 1919.

Taylor, Vincent. *The Formation of the Gospel Tradition: Eight Lectures.* London: Macmillan & Co. Ltd., 1964.

Temple, William. *Christus Veritas: An Essay.* London: Macmillan & Co Ltd., 1954.

The Book of Yahweh, 7th ed.. Abilene, TX: The Houses of Yahweh, 1994.

The Co-founders of Alcoholics Anonymous: Biographical sketches Their last major talks, 1972, 1975.

The Complete Parallel Bible. Oxford: Oxford University Press, 1993.

The Contemporary Parallel New Testament (Eight Translations). NY: Oxford University Press, 1997.

The Dead Sea Scrolls Bible. HarperSanFrancisco, 1999.

The Four Absolutes. Cleveland: Cleveland Central Committee of A.A., n.d.

The New Way of Life. A.A. Cleveland: The Cleveland District Office of Alcoholics Anonymous, n.d.

The Revised English Bible, New Testament

71

The Schocken Bible: Volume I (The Five Books of Moses). NY: Schocken Books, 1995.

The Tidings. March 24, 1943.

The Upper Room (Methodist quarterly periodical which began publishing in April, 1935).

Three Old-timer Clarence Snyder Sponsees and Wive. *Our A.A. Faith Legacy*. FL: Came to Believe Pub., 2005.

Tileston, Mary W. *Daily Strength for Daily Needs*. Boston: Roberts Brothers, 1893.

Tournier, Paul. *The Healing of Persons*. NY: Harper & Row, Publishers, 1965.

_____. *The Person Reborn*. NY: Harper & Row, Publishers, 1966.

Towns, Elmer. Porter, Douglas. *The Ten Greatest Revivals Ever: From Pentecost to the Present*. MI: Servant Publications, 2000.

Troward, Thomas. *The Edinburgh Lectures on Mental Science*. NY: Dodd, Mead & Co., 1909.

Vine's Expository Dictionary of Old and New Testament Words. NY: Fleming H. Revell, 1981.

Walter, Howard A. *Soul Surgery*. Oxford: The Oxford Group, 1928.

Weatherhead, Leslie D. *Psychology and Life*. New York: Abingdon Press, 1935.

_____. *Psychology, Religion, and Healing*. NY: Abingdon-Cokesbury Press, 1951.

Weaver, C. Douglas. *William Marrion Branham: The Healer-Prophet*. GA; Mercer University Press, 2000.

Wells, Amos R. *Expert Endeavor: A Text-book of Christian Endeavor Methods and Principles*. Boston: United Society of Christian Endeavor, 1911.

What Others Think of A.A. Akron: Friday Forum Luncheon Club, circa 1941.

White, William L. *Slaying the Dragon: The History of Addiction Treatment and Recovery in America.* Bloomington, IL: Chestnut Health Systems/Lighthouse Institute, 1998.

Wigglesworth, Smith. *Smith Wigglesworth on Healing*. PA: Whitaker House, 1999.

Willitts, Ethel R. *Healing in Jesus Name*. Crawfordsville, IN: Ethel R. Willitts, Publisher, 1931.

Wilson, Jim. *Healing Through The Power of Christ*. London: James Clarke & Co., Ltd., 1946.

Wilson, Lois. *Lois Remembers*.

Wilson, Bill. *Bill Wilson's Original Story*. Bedford Hills, NY: Stepping Stones Archives, n.d., a manuscript whose individual lines are numbered 1 to 1180.

_____. *Bill W. My First Forty Years*. MN: Hazelden.

About the Author

Dick B. writes books on the spiritual roots of Alcoholics Anonymous. They show how the basic and highly successful biblical ideas used by early AAs can be valuable tools for success in today's A.A. His research can also help the religious and recovery communities work more effectively with alcoholics, addicts, and others involved in Twelve Step programs.

The author is an active, recovered member of A.A.; a retired attorney; and a Bible student. He has sponsored more than one hundred men in their recovery from alcoholism. Consistent with A.A.'s traditions of anonymity, he uses the pseudonym "Dick B."

He has had twenty-eight titles published including: *Dr. Bob and His Library*; *Anne Smith's Journal, 1933-1939*; *The Oxford Group & Alcoholics Anonymous*; *The Akron Genesis of Alcoholics Anonymous*; *The Books Early AAs Read for Spiritual Growth*; *New Light on Alcoholism: God, Sam Shoemaker, and A.A.*; *Courage to Change* (with Bill Pittman); *Cured: Proven Help for Alcoholics and Addicts; The Good Book and The Big Book: A.A.'s Roots in the Bible*; *That Amazing Grace: The Role of Clarence and Grace S. in Alcoholics Anonymous*; *Good Morning!: Quiet Time, Morning Watch, Meditation, and Early A.A.*; *Turning Point: A History of Early A.A.'s Spiritual Roots and Successes, Hope!: The Story of Geraldine D., Alina Lodge & Recovery; Utilizing Early A.A.'s Spiritual Roots for Recovery Today; The Golden Text of A.A.; By the Power of God; God and Alcoholism; Making Known the Biblical History of A.A.; Why Early A.A. Succeeded; Comments of Dick B. at The First Nationwide A.A. History Conference; Henrietta Seiberling: Ohio's Lady with a Cause; and The James Club*. The books have been the subject of newspaper articles and reviews in *Library Journal, Bookstore Journal, The Living Church, Faith at Work, Sober Times, Episcopal Life, Recovery News, Ohioana Quarterly, The PHOENIX*, and *The Saint Louis University Theology Digest*. They are listed in the biographies of major addiction center, religion, and religious history sites. He has published over 150 articles on his subject, most posted on the internet.

Dick is the father of two sons (Ken and Don) and has two granddaughters. As a young man, he did a stint as a newspaper reporter. He attended the University of California, Berkeley, where he received his A.A. degree with Honorable Mention, majored in economics, and was elected to Phi Beta Kappa in his Junior year. In the United States Army, he was an Information-Education Specialist. He received his A.B. and J.D. degrees from Stanford University, and was Case Editor of the Stanford Law Review. Dick became interested in Bible study in his childhood Sunday School and was much inspired by his mother's almost daily study of Scripture. He joined, and was president of, a Community Church affiliated with the United Church of Christ. By 1972, he was studying the origins of the Bible and began traveling abroad in pursuit of that subject. In 1979, he became much involved in a Biblical research, teaching, and fellowship ministry. In his community life, he was president of a merchants' council, Chamber of Commerce, church retirement center, and homeowners' association. He served on a public district board and has held offices in a service club.

In 1986, he was felled by alcoholism, gave up his law practice, and began recovery as a member of the Fellowship of Alcoholics Anonymous. In 1990, his interest in A.A.'s Biblical/Christian roots was sparked by his attendance at A.A.'s International Convention in Seattle. He has traveled widely; researched at archives, and at public and seminary libraries; interviewed scholars, historians, clergy, A.A. "old-timers" and survivors; and participated in programs and conferences on A.A.'s roots.

The author is the owner of Good Book Publishing Company and has several works in progress. Much of his research and writing is done in collaboration with his older son, Ken, an ordained minister, who holds B.A., B.Th., and M.A. degrees. Ken has been a lecturer in New Testament Greek at a Bible college and a lecturer in Fundamentals of Oral Communication at San Francisco State University. Ken is a computer specialist and director of marketing and research in Hawaii ethanol projects.

Dick is a member of the American Historical Association, Research Society on Alcoholism, Alcohol and Drugs History Society, Organization of American Historians, The Association for Medical Education and Research in Substance Abuse, Coalition of Prison Evangelists, Christian Association for Psychological Studies, and International Substance Abuse and Addictions Coalition. He is available for conferences, panels, seminars, and interviews.

Good Book Publishing Company Order Form

(Use this form to order Dick B.'s titles on early A.A.'s roots and successes)

Qty.	Titles by Dick B.	Price
____	*A New Way In*	$19.95 ea. $ _____
____	*A New Way Out*	$19.95 ea. $ _____
____	*Anne Smith's Journal, 1933-1939*	$22.95 ea. $ _____
____	*By the Power of God: A Guide to Early A.A. Groups and Forming Similar Groups Today*	$23.95 ea. $ _____
____	*Cured! Proven Help for Alcoholics and Addicts*	$23.95 ea. $ _____
____	*Dr. Bob and His Library*	$22.95 ea. $ _____
____	*Dr. Bob of Alcoholics Anonymous*	$24.95 ea. $ _____
____	*God and Alcoholism*	$21.95 ea. $ _____
____	*Good Morning! Quiet Time, Morning Watch, Meditation, and Early A.A.*	$22.95 ea. $ _____
____	*Henrietta B. Seiberling*	$20.95 ea. $ _____
____	*Introduction to the Sources and Founding of A.A.*	$22.95 ea. $ _____
____	*Making Known the Biblical History and Roots of Alcoholics Anonymous*	$24.95 ea. $ _____
____	*New Light on Alcoholism: God, Sam Shoemaker, and A.A.*	$24.95 ea. $ _____
____	*Real Twelve Step Fellowship History*	$23.95 ea. $ _____
____	*That Amazing Grace: The Role of Clarence and Grace S. in Alcoholics Anonymous*	$22.95 ea. $ _____
____	*The Akron Genesis of Alcoholics Anonymous*	$23.95 ea. $ _____
____	*The Books Early AAs Read for Spiritual Growth*	$21.95 ea. $ _____
____	*The Conversion of Bill W.*	$23.95 ea. $ _____
____	*The First Nationwide A.A. History Conference*	$22.95 ea. $ _____
____	*The Golden Text of A.A.*	$20.95 ea. $ _____
____	*The Good Book and the Big Book: A.A.'s Roots in the Bible*	$23.95 ea. $ _____
____	*The Good Book-Big Book Guidebook*	$22.95 ea. $ _____
____	*The James Club and the Original A.A. Program's Absolute Essentials*	$23.95 ea. $ _____
____	*The Oxford Group and Alcoholics Anonymous*	$23.95 ea. $ _____
____	*Turning Point: A History of Early A.A.'s Spiritual Roots and Successes*	$29.95 ea. $ _____
____	*Twelve Steps for You*	$21.95 ea. $ _____
____	*Utilizing Early A.A.'s Spiritual Roots for Recovery Today*	$20.95 ea. $ _____
____	*When Early AAs Were Cured and Why*	$23.95 ea. $ _____
____	*Why Early A.A. Succeeded*	$23.95 ea. $ _____

(Order Form continued on the next page)

Good Book Publishing Company Order Form
(continued from the previous page)

Order Subtotal: $ _____

Shipping and Handling (S&H) **: $ _____

(** For Shipping and Handling, please add 10% of the Order Subtotal for U.S. orders or 15% of the Order Subtotal for international orders. The minimum U.S. S&H is $5.60. The minimum S&H for Canada and Mexico is US$ 9.95. The minimum S&H for other countries is US$ 11.95.)

Order Total: $ _____

Credit card: VISA   MasterCard   American Express   Discover   (circle one)

Account number: _____ Exp.: _____

Name: _____ (as it is on your credit card, if using one)

(Company: _____)

Address Line 1: _____

Address Line 2: _____

City: _____ State/Prov.: _____

Zip/Postal Code: _____ Country: _____

Signature: _____ Telephone: _____

Email: _____

No returns accepted. Please mail this Order Form, along with your check or money order (if sending one), to: Dick B., c/o Good Book Publishing Company, PO Box 837, Kihei, HI 96753-0837. Please make your check or money order (if sending one) payable to "Dick B." in U.S. dollars drawn on a U.S. bank. If you have any questions, please phone: 1-808-874-4876 or send an email message to: dickb@dickb.com. Dick B.'s web site: www.DickB.com.

If you would like to purchase Dick B.'s entire 29-volume reference set on early A.A.'s roots and successes (and how those successes may be replicated today) at a substantial discount, please send Dick B. an email message or give him a call.

Paradise Research Publications, Inc.
PO Box 837
Kihei, HI 96753-0837
(808) 874-4876
Email: dickb@dickb.com
URL: http://www.dickb.com/index.shtml
http://www.dickb-blog.com

20922218R00050

Made in the USA
Lexington, KY
22 February 2013